TEAM ORGANIZATION

The Authors

Thomas O. Erb is Associate Professor and Chair, Department of Curriculum and Instruction, School of Education, University of Kansas, Lawrence.

Nancy M. Doda, a former middle school teacher and university professor, is an educational consultant in Burke, Virginia.

The Advisory Panel

Ruth W. Bauer, Eighth Grade Language Arts Teacher, Cheshire, Connecticut

June Russell Gilstad, Educational Consultant, Kokomo, Indiana

Linda D. McDaniel, National Teacher-Trainer for Growing Healthy, Van Buren Middle School, Arkansas

C. Kenneth McEwin, Professor of Curriculum and Instruction, College of Education, Appalachian State University, Boone, North Carolina

Daniel Paul, Professor of Elementary Curriculum and Methods, Hope College, Holland, Michigan

Denny L. Schillings, Social Studies Teacher, Homewood-Flossmoor High School, Flossmoor, Illinois

Sandra Silver, Principal, Paul Bunyan Elementary School, Bemidji, Minnesota

Judith Wilhelmy, Reading Specialist, Page School, Ayer, Massachusetts

TEAM ORGANIZATION:
Promise—Practices and Possibilities

Thomas O. Erb
Nancy M. Doda

nea PROFESSIONAL LIBRARY
National Education Association
Washington, D.C.

Authors' Acknowledgments

Preparing this manuscript has indeed been an exemplary team endeavor. Individual teachers, administrators, and our colleagues have joined us with their examples of fine teamwork. We are especially indebted to those teachers and administrators in over three dozen schools in nine states who have shared with us their experiences with teaming. We are grateful for our families who continued to love and support us during the long hours of writing. We also wish to acknowledge the mentor who has helped us see teaming in new ways, Professor Paul George.

—T. O. E.
N. M. D.

Library of Congress Cataloging-in-Publication Data

Erb, Thomas Owen.
    Team organization : promise—practices and possibilities / Thomas O. Erb, Nancy M. Doda
        p.   cm. — (Analysis and action series)
    Bibliography: p.
    Includes index.
    ISBN 0-8106-3075-3
    1. Teaching teams—United States.   I. Doda, Nancy.   II. Title.
III. Series.
LB1029.T4E73   1989
371.1'48—dc20   89-33741
                                                                            CIP

CONTENTS

Chapter 1

TEAM ORGANIZATION: WHAT IS IT? WHY BOTHER?

A year ago I was fighting this thing tooth and nail. The "Bright Boys" were trying to force something else down our throats. But, you know, teaming is the best thing that ever happened to my teaching.

Math teacher, Missouri

If they do away with teaming, I'll quit teaching.

English teacher, Kansas

What is teaming? How has it transformed the lives of these and other teachers and students? Teaming or, more formally, inter-disciplinary team organization is a way of organizing teachers and students into small communities for teaching and learning. Though they vary in composition and size, teams are generally comprised of from two to five teachers who represent diverse subject areas, but who share a common planning period to prepare for the teaching of a common set of students. Most often these teachers also share a common block schedule and adjacent classrooms.

Common planning time is built into the team members' regular workdays. In addition to teaching several classes of students daily and having an individual planning period, these teamed teachers share a team meeting time. The concept of teaming also requires these teachers to share a *common set of students*. For example, the social studies, science, mathematics, and English teachers on a team teach the same students throughout the day.

In combination with the sharing of common planning time and students, two other factors facilitate the operation of teaching teams. The first of these is a *block teaching schedule*. In a pure block, four teamed teachers would share a four-period block of time during which they would have all of their students in class. For example, for the first four periods of the day all their students would be under their jurisdiction, being taught by the various team members. The final facilitative element is *common space*.

7

This term refers to the practice of placing the teamed teachers in adjacent classrooms or, in more modern structures, in a single pod. When teamed teachers are in proximity to one another, they gain control over a team area that is larger than a single classroom and includes adjacent hall space as well as the separate classrooms involved.

On the surface, team organization is deceptively simple. It involves only four basic elements: a common group of students, common planning time, a common block teaching schedule, and a common team area. Yet when teachers take full advantage of these four elements, their work life is fundamentally changed, as is the support system for students. Communications patterns within a school change, teachers' involvement in decision making improves, instruction better serves the needs of students, the curriculum is transformed, and teachers find the practice of their profession more rewarding.

It sounds too good to be true. Teaming must be another educational fad, promoted by some highly paid California consultant! Not so. The purpose of this book is to show how teaming is currently achieving these results in hundreds of schools across America. Of course, teaming, like any other education practice, can be done poorly as well as effectively. Another purpose of this book is to share the experiences of those who have been successful with team organization. The problems and the pitfalls will be examined, as will the promise of a better way to organize teachers to effectively carry out their roles as professional educators.

TEAMING'S RELATIONSHIP TO SUCCESSFUL SCHOOLS

After heading an eight-year study of 1,350 teachers, 8,624 parents, and 17,163 students in 1,016 classrooms at all three levels of public education (i.e., elementary, middle school/junior high, and secondary), Goodlad concluded the following:

> To the unrelenting advocates of departmentalization, on the one hand, and the self-contained classroom, on the other, my response has to be, "A plague on both your houses." Surely there are creative ways to secure some of the advantages of both departmentalization and self-contained classrooms without the weaknesses of either. (34,* p. 308)

---

*Numbers in parentheses appearing in the text refer to the Bibliography beginning on page 123.

Teacher Autonomy

Though Goodlad (34) did not explicitly use the term *interdisciplinary team organization*, he left little doubt that some creative blend of the two most common organizational patterns used in schools would be better than the prevailing practice. He found fault with education practices that could not be adequately corrected unless teachers were organized into interdisciplinary teams. Arguing that schools were too large to meet the needs of most students, he called for either smaller schools or "schools-within-schools" to effectively reduce the size of elementary schools with more than 300 students and junior highs and senior highs with more than 600. Goodlad based his case on both curricular matters and student welfare. He called for more flexible approaches to meeting students' needs. He also called for more diversified teaching, more flexible scheduling of instructional experiences, more multiaged grouping of students, and more mastery learning. His proposals for giving teachers more professional autonomy would be facilitated by interdisciplinary team organization.

Among those who have spent a considerable amount of time studying schools, Goodlad is not alone in calling for educational improvements that can occur only if teachers work in teams. Boyer (10), after a two-and-one-half-year study of American secondary schools, argued for the need to provide more curricular cohesion, a task that is virtually impossible unless teachers of different subjects communicate with each other on a regular basis. Boyer called explicitly for more teacher collegiality and common planning time. He felt that the interaction fostered by common planning time was necessary to guarantee more teacher autonomy in the area of instruction. Only by working in teams with shared space and block schedules could teachers free themselves from the tyranny of bell schedules and the limitations of traditional classroom spaces. Teaming also facilitates the flexible grouping of students, which is necessary to reduce the use of the discredited practice of tracking students (71).

Yet a third observer of American schools found traditional organizational patterns too inflexible to provide a truly appropriate education for students. Focusing on the instructional triangle of students, teachers, and subject matter in over 100 classrooms, Sizer (68) reiterated several of the points made by Goodlad and Boyer:

9

more integration of subject matter, more cross-age grouping of students, more flexible ability grouping of students (as opposed to tracking), and bigger blocks of time to increase flexibility are needed. Sizer also called for schools-within-schools to provide for more effective interaction of students and teachers with subject matter. He, too, thought that more teacher autonomy is essential to improving learning in secondary schools.

A Coalition of Essential Schools has been formed to test some of Sizer's ideas in secondary schools. Several of these secondary schools are experimenting with team organization characterized by large blocks of teaching time, flexible grouping of students, interdisciplinary teaching, and teachers planning together (11).

After observing team organization in over two dozen schools, Erb (25) argued that team organization provides the means by which teachers can gain greater control of the teaching-learning environment. In this manner, teachers can more productively respond to diverse learner needs. Consequently, teaming has greater potential for improving the instruction of students than any of the "effective" teaching formulas being imposed on teachers by well-meaning but overzealous reformers.

Collegiality

In addition to teacher autonomy, the need for more collegiality among teachers is a major theme to emerge in the 1980s. Comparing the results from competitive and cooperative workplaces, Rosenholtz (66) found that improved teaching and a greater sense of professional pride are associated with collegial arrangements, such as team organization. Barth (5) made the case that encouraging more collaboration at the individual school level is a necessary step in closing the gap between the way schools are and the way educators would like them to be. The Tyes (75) argued that schools cannot be improved as long as teachers remain isolated from each other in their work settings. Their research demonstrated that collegial interdependence among teachers, which in turn can lead to shared, schoolwide decision making, is necessary for effective school reform.

In a very important study of collegiality in school settings, Little (58) found that in successful schools, teachers valued and participated in the norms of collegiality and continuous improvement.

They pursued a greater range of professional interactions (e.g., talk about instruction, structured observation, and shared planning) with both their colleagues and administrators. They also did so with greater frequency, in more locations, and with a more concrete and precise shared language than did teachers in schools that were not functioning as well.

After reviewing nearly sixty articles dealing with the concept of teaming and collaboration, other researchers (45) have concluded that collaboration is essential if teachers are to feel job satisfaction and to be provided with opportunities for continued growth. Our current understanding of collaboration and cooperative learning provides a sound basis for the use of interdisciplinary teams in schools.

Efficacy

Teacher autonomy and collegiality lead to a third factor that is associated with teacher effectiveness: efficacy. A teacher's sense of efficacy or power to influence student learning is a complex concept. It involves not only a personal sense of competence but also a general sense that teachers can influence student learning, regardless of various student backgrounds. Doda, writing in Ashton and Webb (4), compared teacher efficacy in teamed and nonteamed middle schools and found that teachers who were organized as teams—in which they worked together in the same part of the building, shared the same students, worked with the same daily teaching schedule, and shared the same planning room with common resources and supplies—showed higher levels of confidence in their own sense of teaching competence. Ashton and Webb (4) have shown that teacher efficacy is clearly tied to student achievement in the areas of mathematics and language. Their study demonstrated the empirical link between team organization and improved student achievement, mediated through teachers' sense of efficacy.

After their extensive review of the literature on teaming, Arhar, Johnston, and Markle (2) claimed that while teaming arrangements are not sufficient to cause collaboration among teachers, they are an essential prerequisite for such cooperation to occur. This cooperative behavior in turn leads to shared decision-making opportunities in a teamed setting. It is these shared decision-making opportunities that are associated with a greater sense of power and control on the part of teachers.

Studies of Successful Middle Grades Schools

Though team organization can contribute to teacher autonomy, collegiality, and efficacy at any level of schooling, to date it has been most often practiced in grades four through nine. Several studies of middle grades schools have emphasized the role of teams in the success of those schools. Lipsitz (57) discovered that the successful schools in her study provided small, stable reference groups for students and collegiality for teachers. Where teaming was used, student alienation and teacher isolation were reduced. George and Oldaker (32) found that interdisciplinary team organization, along with some other organizational arrangements often found in middle schools, is associated with improved student achievement, school discipline, student personal development, general school climate, faculty morale, and parental support. Doda (18) described interdisciplinary teams as one of four factors that interact to create effective school cultures. Johnston and Ramos de Perez (46) identified four climates of effective middle grades schools: academic, social-emotional, organizational, and physical. Each of these is enhanced by the functioning of interdisciplinary teams.

In a study that focused exclusively on the impact of team organization on teachers, Erb (24) documented four differences between the ways teachers on teams function as opposed to the ways of those who are not so organized. First, teamed teachers engage in more frequent and more in-depth professional discussions. Not only do these discussions occur more often with colleagues concerning students, instruction, curriculum, and staff development, but also they occur more often with counselors, special educators, administrators, and parents. Second, this increased communication leads to more teacher involvement in the decision-making processes of the school, which are more collegial than those found in schools in which teachers tend to be isolated from each other. Third, not only do teachers have more involvement in the process of decision making, but also they tend to have greater influence over those decisions that most directly affect their teaching. Finally, teachers find that working on teams makes teaching more rewarding. Team teaching provides a supportive environment that overcomes the isolation that most teachers experience when they are working in self-contained or departmentalized classrooms.

SUMMARY

It is clear that team arrangements reduce teacher isolation, increase satisfaction, and improve individual teachers' sense of efficacy. (2, p. 25)

Of the many suggestions offered for reforming American public education in the 1990s, team organization is one of the most powerful. During the past decade, teaming has emerged as one of the few substantial reform concepts and practices with the capacity to transform the way schools operate for teachers and students. Because it facilitates communication and collaboration, teaming is an enabling reform that fosters collegiality and interpersonal affiliation. In this way team organization is far more than an instructional innovation. It changes the professional and interpersonal dynamics of schools for everyone involved.

Not only do teaming arrangements improve the professional lives of teachers, but also a growing body of research points to the conclusion that teaming leads to improved student performance. The relationship between teaming and student outcomes is not a direct one. While teaming does not cause teachers to become committed to engaging in teacher-student relationships that facilitate growth and individual student development, it is certain that teaming gives them the ability to translate this commitment into action (3).

Not surprisingly, such a powerful reform requires disciplined planning if it is to be implemented well. Fortunately, a sufficient number of schools have experienced trials and successes with teaming to supply others with valuable guidance. For those seeking to implement team organization, and for others hoping to revitalize their currently existing programs, this monograph will provide practical suggestions based on this experience.

Chapter 2

THE ENABLING FACTORS: GETTING STARTED RIGHT

Long before the first team meetings take place, careful planning must occur to lay the foundation for successful teaming. A number of administrative decisions need to be made, often with teacher input, prior to the implementation of team organization. Even after teams are established, issues related to how the teams will fit into the overall operation of the school will continue to exist. This chapter focuses on these contextual matters that need special attention in order to facilitate the work of the teams. The next chapter will concentrate on the face-to-face encounters that will occur on teams after they are formed and functioning.

PLANNING TO IMPLEMENT TEAMS

Staffing Considerations

Though teachers new to teaming often express concerns about how compatible they will be with their teammates, successful teamwork requires a variety of strengths and personalities. Four people who are the best of friends may make a great bridge club, but they will not necessarily make a good team of teachers. One secret of successful teaming is the bringing together of people with different backgrounds, perspectives, and subject matter specializations who can contribute to the growth of other team members and to the collective strength of the team. In setting up teams, several factors can be taken into account to ensure that team members are *not* clones of each other.

The most obvious factor in setting up interdisciplinary teams is that the team members will bring different subject matter specializations to the team setting. The specific combinations of subject matter expertise vary greatly from team to team. For example, on some four-person teams each teacher will be responsible for a different subject area: language arts, mathematics, social studies, and science. On other teams one teacher might teach two subjects, such as social studies and mathematics or science and reading. On yet other teams the members may each teach one basic subject, and everyone shares the teaching of a remaining subject, such as reading or mathematics. Teamed teachers can even divide up in unique ways a subject taught by several team members. For example, if all team members teach social studies, they can decide to split up the social studies topics so that each one can teach those units that he or she prefers. That way students experience the whole social studies program, but each teacher is responsible for only a part of the total course.

In setting up teams, administrators are naturally restricted by the certification endorsements held by the various faculty members. Teachers with elementary certification can generally function more flexibly on teams because they are often certified to teach several basic subjects. More and more, teachers with middle-level certificates are certified to teach at least two subjects. However, teachers who hold only secondary certificates are typically limited to teaching the one subject for which they hold endorsement. When selecting teams, the certifications held by the faculty will play a significant role.

Beyond the legal matter of certification, several factors of teacher preference should be taken into account in setting up teams. The first of these factors is teacher preference of subject(s) to teach. The fact that an elementary-certified teacher can *legally* teach all the basic subjects does not mean that that teacher feels comfortable teaching several different subjects at the required grade level. On the other hand, a teacher who is currently certified in one or two specified subjects at the middle or secondary level might be interested in adding a new endorsement to teach in yet another area. For example, a teacher certified in secondary science might wish to expand her opportunities by adding a second endorsement in mathematics so that she can teach both subjects in a teamed setting. Regardless of the current certification status of the various faculty members, their preferences of subjects to teach should be considered when teams are either organized for the first time or reorganized.

The teams to be organized in a given school often vary in several ways, particularly with respect to grade level and size. Depending on the grade level configuration of the building, a teacher may wish to teach at the fifth or sixth grade level rather than at the seventh or eighth grade level. Such preferences should be taken into account. In some schools grade-level teams may coexist with one or two multiage teams. Once again, teacher preference must be considered when deciding whether to place a person on a single-grade team or a multiage team. In addition, it is not uncommon to find two-person, three-person, and four- or five-person teams existing side by side in a single building. Team size is often influenced by enrollment figures (for example, when fifty students are left over and only a two-person team can be justified under the current budget) or student needs (as when a two-person team is set up at the sixth grade level to reduce the number of adults that these less mature students would have to deal with). When options as to team size are available in a building, the person setting up the teams should consider teacher wishes regarding the size of team to work on.

Though we cautioned above that the best of friends do not necessarily make the best teammates, it is legitimate to consider teacher preference regarding whom they would like to work with and whom they would prefer *not* to work with. Asking teachers to indicate any individuals whom they feel they could not work with is a wise measure that can head off future problems with the staffing of teams. A Staff Preference Sheet (Figure 2.1) is useful for collecting and organizing much information relevant to the staffing of teams.

With the information contained in the Staff Preference Sheet, the person selecting teams may have all the information that can be taken into account in assigning teachers to teams. Even in large schools with three or more teams per grade level, the factors discussed above might put so many restrictions on assigning people to teams that no additional information is useful. However, some schools have attempted to go beyond the factors discussed thus far to include information about teacher psychological type, leadership style, and/or teaching style. Several instruments are available that can provide information about these dimensions of teacher personality. Even if knowledge of these factors provides information overload at the time of team selection, once teams are formed it can be very helpful for team members to share this information as they are getting to know their teammates. Consequently, there may be value in administering one or more of these instruments so

16

Figure 2.1

Staff Preference Sheet

In the near future, we will develop teams for the coming school year. Please fill out the form below and return it to me by 3:00 March 20. An envelope is provided to ensure confidentiality. This form will be reviewed by the principals. It is not shared with other staff members or the central administration.

Name: _____

1. I plan to return to the district next year. ☐ Yes ☐ No

2. List all areas of certification:

   _____   _____

   _____   _____

   Temporary certification:

   _____   _____

   _____   _____

3. Grade-level preference:

   First choice: ____ Second choice: ____ Third choice: ____

4. Rank in order the subjects you prefer to teach:

   1. _____   3. _____

   2. _____   4. _____

5. Rank in order the team configuration you prefer:

   ☐ one person   ☐ three person   ☐ five person

   ☐ two person   ☐ four person   ☐ multigrade

6. List persons you would like to team with:

   _____   _____

   _____   _____

   _____   _____

7. List persons you would not like to team with:

   _____   _____

   _____   _____

_____

Source: Developed by Nipher Middle School, Kirkwood, Missouri. Reprinted with permission.

17

that teachers can become more knowledgeable about themselves and their teammates.

Several of the various systems for identifying and describing different personality types and leadership styles are summarized below. References are given for each one so that readers can gather further information about any system that they may wish to consider. A good overview of several systems, including some not discussed here, has been published in *Marching to Different Drummers* (37).

The *Myers-Briggs Type Indicator* (55, 60, 61, 62) and the *Keirsey Temperament Sorter* (48) are based on Jung's (47) theory of psychological type. These instruments divide people into sixteen personality types based on four dimensions: extroversion-introversion, sensing-intuition, thinking-feeling, and judging-perceiving. These sixteen types can be analyzed in several ways:

1. Temperament
   a. Dionysian (sensing perceiving)
   b. Epimethean (sensing judging)
   c. Promethean (intuitive thinking)
   d. Apollonian (intuitive feeling)

2. Decision-making orientation
   a. Impersonal fact analyzers (sensing thinking)
   b. Relationship fact analyzers (sensing feeling)
   c. Social possibility analyzers (intuitive feeling)
   d. Impersonal theory analyzers (intuitive thinking)

The *Gregorc Style Delineator* (35, 36) defines people's ways of transacting with their environment based on the intersection of two dimensions: concrete-abstract and sequential-random. Four personality types result:

1. Concrete sequential
2. Abstract random
3. Abstract sequential
4. Concrete random

The *S-C Teaching Inventory* (8) defines five teaching styles based on the interaction of two dimensions: high and low student orientation and high and low task orientation. The five resulting teaching styles are these:

1. Teaching focus
2. Friendship and support focus
3. Do-my-job focus
4. Compromising focus
5. Learning focus

The *Learning Styles Inventory* (53, 54) divides people's learning styles into four types based on the intersection of two dimensions: a perception dimension with concrete and random at the poles and a processing dimension with active and reflective at the poles. These four styles result:

1. Reflective sensor/feelers (divergers)
2. Reflective thinkers (assimilators)
3. Thinking doers (convergers)
4. Doing sensor/feelers (accommodators)

The information that these instruments generate about teachers can be very useful in helping them better understand themselves and their teammates. Such information can promote greater appreciation of the differences among people in the ways they encounter the world, process information, make decisions, and teach. It can also help teachers understand the potential for conflict among people with different styles. Consequently, teachers will be better prepared to work with their teammates in a spirit of understanding and cooperation.

Ultimately, the decisions regarding team staffing must rest with a person who has an overview of the whole school. This person is most often the building principal. Even with the careful solicitation of all the types of information discussed, this person must finally trust his or her judgment regarding who should be placed with whom. We do not yet know enough to override the professional judgment of building principals who carefully weigh the information available and then make the decisions that they deem best for the school.

Team Leadership

Teaming is essentially a collegial endeavor. A team leader, then, is not a line position in the sense that other team members "report" to the team leader. On the contrary, a team leader functions more as a facilitator of the team's work. For small groups to be

19

successful, different individuals need to take responsibility for the diverse tasks that must be carried out. Successful teams often define several roles that need to be fulfilled. Though teams vary in defining these roles, each team needs to be clear about what tasks it expects to be done and who will be responsible for seeing that each one is completed. Often teams are guided in their discussions of these roles by job descriptions created at the district level (Figure 2.2) or the building level (Figure 2.3). However, since these roles must finally be worked out within each team, more will be said about them in the next chapter.

In addition to fulfilling roles within the structure of the team, the team leader usually represents the team to the rest of the school organization. Therefore, schools often define the role of the team leader in relationship to roles outside of the team—most commonly, those of the administration and the team coordinator. Figure 2.2 presents the job descriptions that were created in the Parkway (Missouri) School District. The team leader has responsibilities that relate to both the internal functioning (e.g., setting agendas, keeping logs, coordinating the calendar) and the external functioning (e.g., communicating with department chairs, attending team leader meetings) of the team. As is often the case, here the team leader's role is rotated throughout the year among all team members.

Figure 2.2

Job Descriptions/Teaming Roles

ADMINISTRATION

Program goals
Schedule/rooms/lockers/planning areas
Team and department identity
"Morale" of nonteam members
Review team meeting logs
Monitor student progress—pretest/posttest
Monitor team progress
Guide in-service
Plan upcoming school year
Select teams and team leaders

Figure 2.2 (Continued)

TEAMING PROJECT LEADER

Help in the selection of teams and team leaders
Develop team dynamics (communication, running meetings,   etc.)
Schedule consultants (e.g., discipline, interdisciplinary,
    computer. . . .)
Establish "team" goals
Work with administration on in-service (follow-up activities)
Coordinate "skill of the week" (study skills, vocabulary, themes)
    and other projects
Field trips, etc.
Liaison to building activities
    –Attendance
    –Budget
    –Library
    –Computer room
    –SSD
    –Counseling
Try to include electives
Handle conflicts between department and team meetings
Organize weekly meeting of rotated team leaders

ROTATED TEAM LEADERS

Set agenda for meetings
Implement projects
Schedule classes and events (e.g., movies, speakers. . . .)
Complete team planning log (keep notebook)
Coordinate tests, lessons. . . .
Organize phone calls and parent and student conferences
Lead team to make continuous, thorough analysis and
    evaluation of each student's progress
Keep department chair informed of problems or concerns the
    team has
Attend weekly meeting of rotated team leaders

TEAM MEMBERS

Attend meetings
Participate in discussion (share ideas)
Follow through on decisions made
Maintain a spirit of trust, collaboration, and confidentiality with
    each other
Aid in achieving team goals

Source: Developed by Parkway South Junior High School, Manchester, Missouri. Reprinted with permission.

As they prepared to initiate teaming, the staff of the Leawood (Kansas) Middle School defined six roles related to team organization (Figure 2.3). The external role is that of grade-level coordinator who provides coordination across teams at a given grade level and represents grade-level interests to the administration. The team leader has seven functions and is the bridge between the team and the rest of the school. Four other roles are defined within the team: in addition to the roles of team facilitator, communicator, and recorder, the Leawood staff created the role of esteem builder. This person is responsible for seeing to it that the whole issue of building self-esteem among team members—students as well as teachers—is not overlooked.

A question that often comes up relates to how team leaders should be chosen and how long they should serve. There is no one clear answer to this question. In some successful situations the team leaders are chosen by their principals and serve in a permanent capacity. In other schools the leaders are chosen by the team members and serve extended terms of office. In yet other viable situations the team leadership is rotated at regular intervals among all the members of the team.

In determining which arrangement would be best for you, such factors as school size, stage of team development, functions assigned to team leaders, and whether or not team leaders are to be compensated need to be considered. In larger schools where the team leaders collectively form an administrative advisory council with the principal, the principal may wish to appoint leadership whom she or he can work with effectively. In other settings where team coordinators and principals meet regularly with whole teams, it may be better to let the choice of team leader rest with the team membership. Often schools just starting out with team organization choose to rotate the role of team leader so that all team members can experience the role and come to appreciate the responsibilities associated with it. If the team leader's role is not compensated, that might suggest rotating it among the team members. In such cases sharing equitably in the responsibilities associated with team membership is a factor. In situations where a large part of the team leader's role is defined by responsibilities external to the team, more permanent appointments might be in order so that outsiders will know who the team leader is. Though there is no one right answer associated with successful teaming, it

22

Figure 2.3

Responsibilities of Team Personnel

GRADE-LEVEL COORDINATOR

1. Work with grade-level team members to create and establish goals.
2. Coordinate grade-level curriculum matters.
3. Distribute/utilize grade-level materials and maintain a working inventory.
4. Act as liaison between grade-level teams and exploratory team members.
5. Organize textbook orders and be responsible, when directed, for dissemination of textbooks and materials.
6. Assist with organization and administration of standardized tests.
7. Help in planning and arranging grade-level assemblies.
8. Help in planning and implementing teacher advisory activities.
9. Work with the PTO liaison person for PTO-sponsored and -related activities.
10. Provide regular communication with administrators for team concerns, weekly summary notes, and other team-related information.
11. Cochair cross-team meetings and ensure that teams are treated equally.
12. Be responsible for budget development for specific grade-level line items.
13. Arrange special services referrals/screenings.
14. Work with substitute teachers for team members to assure maximum utilization of their services.
15. Work with administration in arranging quarterly club rotations.
16. Oversee production of the team newsletters.
17. Assure that invited guests are provided with all on-site courtesies and that follow-up notes are sent to guests.
18. Provide administration with the quarterly roles and responsibilities of individual team members.
19. Act as liaison for grade-level teams with the District Middle School Director.
20. Assist administration in selection of teaching personnel for their grade-level teams.
21. Assist counselors with student schedule changes and maintain accurate records of students' schedules.
22. Identify and organize "team skill(s) of the week" and assure their implementation within the team.

Figure 2.3 (Continued)

TEAM LEADER

1. Be responsible for external and internal team communication.
2. Oversee all individual team meetings and work with the Team Facilitator to create meeting agendas.
3. Be the Instructional Leader for the team and help provide/identify professional growth opportunities for team members.
4. Oversee production of the team newsletter.
5. Lead the team to make continuous, thorough analysis and evaluation of each student's progress.
6. Cochair cross-team meetings with the Grade-Level Coordinator.
7. Assist the administration and the Grade-Level Coordinator in the selection of team teaching personnel.

Note: The following team positions are elected/assigned on a quarterly basis.

TEAM FACILITATOR

1. Work with the Team Leader to create agendas for team meetings and chair these meetings.
2. Be directly responsible for production of the team newsletter.
3. Coordinate and chair all team/parent conferences.

COMMUNICATOR

1. Be responsible for all team communication with parents.
2. Maintain a log of parent contacts in the team notebook.
3. Communicate all schedule changes to parents.

RECORDER

1. Maintain the team notebook.
2. Maintain and consistently update the team calendar.
3. Arrange for and distribute all necessary forms and copied material which the team will need.
4. Provide administration, counselors, and team members with weekly summary notes of the team meetings.

ESTEEM BUILDER

1. Be responsible for activities which build the self-esteem of individual students (and groups of students) within the specific team. This will include both in-school positive reinforcement and communication with parents, staff, and news media.

Source: Developed by Leawood (Kansas) Middle School. Reprinted with permission.

is important for people in each school setting to examine their own situation and reach a local decision on selecting team leaders.

It should be clear that there is no one way to define the roles that need to be carried out on a team. It should be equally clear that these roles do need to be defined. Leaving the issue of team leadership to chance is a recipe for failure. Conscious thought needs to be given to defining team roles. These roles also need to be evaluated periodically. If the functions that were originally decided on are found to be flawed, then they need to be changed. But just waiting "for leadership to emerge" will lead to confusion and frustration.

Staff Development Considerations

Switching from a departmentalized or self-contained classroom arrangement to team organization represents a major shift in the way teachers are organized to carry out their professional functions. Though the concept of team organization in schools is at least two decades old, if your school has not been organized that way before, changing to teaming will constitute a major innovation in your setting. Such a change will not succeed without careful planning for staff development. Board edicts or administrative mandates will not suffice. Staff development to prepare for establishing team organization needs to begin no later than early during the school year *prior* to the scheduled implementation date. It must continue intensely during the first year of implementation and periodically thereafter.

We have been helped to understand the process of school change by the work of Hall and others (38, 39, 41) who developed the Concerns-Based Adoption Model (C–BAM). In all, they described six stages of concern that faculties go through when they attempt to implement programmatic innovations. Teachers' concerns tend to change as the process of change is occurring. Briefly, these six stages of concern are the following:

Stage I	Needing information
Stage II	Dealing with personal concerns
Stage III	Dealing with management questions
Stage IV	Focusing on consequences
Stage V	Dealing with collaboration
Stage VI	Refocusing

25

This stages of concern model is confirmed repeatedly in staff development efforts by the fact that the first step, supplying information about teaming, leads teachers to express a number of personal concerns about team organization.

At the very least, the first three stages of concern must be dealt with in preparing teachers to implement teaming. The first, and easiest, part of staff development will be to explain the concept of team organization and the rationale for implementing it. This knowledge level of staff development should also include an explanation of how it is envisioned that teaming will fit with the rest of the school program (e.g., elective areas of the curriculum, homeroom program, extracurricular program). The experience of those schools moving into team organization suggests that carrying out this first aspect of staff development will lead right into the second aspect.

Those planning staff development must not overlook the need to deal with teachers' affective concerns. The staff development process must legitimize these concerns regarding the move to teaming. Failure to do so will not minimize them. On the contrary, they will only be magnified and become barriers to implementation. Chief among the concerns that teachers express about teaming are "Will I get along with all of my teammates?" and "How will teaming affect the way that I teach?" In preteaming workshops, one building staff generated forty-four concerns that they had about implementing teaming (Figure 2.4). Checking this list of concerns, you can see that most of them relate to personal concerns (Stage II) about teaming, just as the C–BAM model predicts. In May of the first year of teaming these same faculty members were again asked to list their concerns. This time their list ran to thirty items (Figure 2.5).

However, in May their concerns dealt mostly with management issues (Stage III), not personal ones. Far from undermining staff development, acknowledging the very real concerns of teachers and dealing with them will open up the communications process and advance the cause of change.

Since teaming requires teachers to relate to each other, to support staff, and to parents in new ways, attention must be given to both teaming skills and teaming practices. Teaming skills can be categorized in various ways. One way to classify teaming skills includes (1) group problem-solving skills, (2) team-building and

26

Figure 2.4

Concerns of Teachers As Team Organization Begins
(Early Fall)

1. That one or two will "carry the load," not all will contribute to the planning.
2. Teachers practicing "passive resistance" to team concept.
3. Teachers on a team who do not understand how to work on a team.
4. Personality conflicts between teachers could hurt the process. People need to have the attitude that they will try to overcome petty differences.
5. If I am a "floater," how would I work in a team? Out of a team? Building unit? Administration direction?
6. Being on a team with some teachers who have discipline problems.
7. I only hope all team members go into this program with a positive attitude. It will work if everyone "feels" it will work.
8. Personality incompatibility could make a long year.
9. Some not willing to compromise for the good of the team.
10. Role of the exploratory teacher.
11. Being pushed aside as inexperienced.
12. Unwillingness to listen to ideas.
13. Personality conflicts.
14. Leadership roles.
15. Assertive discipline.
16. Consistency among team members.
17. All work (falling) on team leader.
18. Getting along with other faculty.
19. Dealing with the discipline problems.
20. Classroom planning (planning period).
21. Being able to cover designated material in a given time slot.
22. Weak or ineffective team leader.
23. A member who is inflexible or isolates him/herself from the rest of the team.
24. What if you are the only strong person teamed with weaker people?
25. What if you are teamed with someone who has a closed mind?
26. Will one teacher, "the strong one," take all discipline for the group?
27. Weak people or person on team —how to solve it.
28. I understand our teams will be set for us. What if I am teamed with someone I find I have a hard time working with?
29. How are fine arts to be worked in?
30. Personality incompatibility could pose a problem.
31. Students should be assigned by counselors, not team members.

Figure 2.4 (Continued)

32. What if I can't get along with team members?
33. How do students, if necessary, switch teams?
34. Cliques among the teams.
35. Not utilizing team planning time effectively.
36. The quiet, unassuming teacher remaining quiet and unassuming.
37. Teachers may not plan well together.
38. Teachers may not be flexible.
39. To understand all aspects of the problem, personality, intellectual, devoutness, etc., by all involved, parents as well.
40. Teachers may not plan well together, if there is a feeling of competition or insecurity.
41. Personality incompatibility.
42. Teachers may not be committed to the ideas of teaming.
43. That as a special educator I will have time to interact and communicate with the teams of the students I work with. That the number of teams I need to communicate with is manageable.
44. Since I have been in a team before, I do not have any team-related concerns.

Source: Bingham Middle Magnet School, Kansas City, Missouri. Reprinted with permission.

Figure 2.5

Concerns of Teachers After Team Implementation (Late Spring)

1. *In your opinion*, do you feel we can be true to both philosophies of being middle *and* magnet?
2. Infusion of magnet theme in middle school setting.
3. More information needed on interdisciplinary units: How many? How important? Who leads?
4. What is the role of a department structure in the middle school?
5. Should there be a general course or specifics offered—i.e., general science or some advanced course like biology?
6. Should there be groups like gifted and slow learning?
7. Our organizational plan has blocks of time for the sixth grade, but then goes to hour time slots for the seventh and eighth (for next year). Is there some logic here I have missed?
8. It is difficult dealing with the level of maturity of 7th and 8th grade. My previous experience has been on senior high level. Any suggestions?
9. Teaming is so important to the middle school. Yet how do you bring teaching philosophies that are so far apart to some middle ground for the good of the team?

Figure 2.5 (Continued)

10. What is the importance of the difference between the middle school "concept" and the junior high school? What statistics prove one is better than the other? What are the *motivations* for having one rather than the other? *How precisely* and importantly might any *one* teacher be affected by *one* (junior high) or the *other* (middle school) organization?
11. At what age, generally, does a child begin to show criminal tendencies?
12. Should the teacher display a fatherly or motherly behavior?
13. Discipline.
14. Effective interdisciplinary planning.
15. Discipline.
16. Teaching strategies.
17. Support from administration.
18. What types of curriculum do most middle schools offer in the various subject areas? Since we are math/science, should we offer biology, algebra, etc.?
19. What resources would you recommend (bookwise) to assist with team teaching in middle schools?
20. I feel very strongly that team teachers should constructively criticize each other's teaching. What is the best way to initiate this in a "resistant" setting?
21. There seems to be a fear of staff members that having to teach sixth grade is a punishment! Also, long-time staff members appear to resent the change from junior high to middle school!
22. I would like to know specifics about middle school concepts and how and why they conflict with some magnet concepts.
23. How the special education student will fit into the general scope of things as it relates to the philosophy of the middle school. . . .
24. How many fine arts (vocal and instrumental) teachers should be staffed for the three grade levels so that there will be equal exposure for students in those three grade levels?
25. I need ideas for positive forms of discipline.
26. What can I do to motivate the class so that I don't keep hearing "I'm bored," and "This is stupid," no matter what activities I have?
27. How can I promote better interpersonal relationships among the students? They are so on edge and explode in an attack on each other at the slightest incident.
28. How can we get the parents more involved in their children's work?
29. Middle school scheduling—how can it be a smooth process?
30. Extra activities and time problems—how can they be resolved?

Source: Bingham Middle Magnet School, Kansas City, Missouri. Reprinted with permission.

maintenance skills, (3) interpersonal skills, and (4) intrapersonal skills (Figure 2.6). Not all teachers bring the same background to teaming. Consequently, they may not all need the same skill-building experiences. However, it is safe to assume that teachers will need some staff development time to work on those skills with which they think they need more practice.

Figure 2.6

Skills Taught in School Team Training

PROBLEM-SOLVING SKILLS:

    a. Brainstorming
    b. Clarifying
    c. Prioritizing
    d. Checking for consensus
    e. Action planning

TEAM-BUILDING AND MAINTENANCE SKILLS:

    a. Establishing norms
    b. Building open agendas
    c. Implementing "rail road" concept
    d. Being knowledgeable of group process and dynamics

INTERPERSONAL SKILLS:

    a. Facilitating communication among team members by teaching
        1. Active listening
        2. Giving and accepting positive feedback
        3. Conflict resolution
        4. Risk taking
    b. Heightening self-awareness
    c. Sharpening introspective skills

INTRAPERSONAL SKILLS:

    a. Managing stress
    b. Setting goals
    c. Developing confidence/self-esteem
    d. Dealing with positive attention

Source: Developed by the Shawnee Mission (Kansas) Public Schools. Reprinted with permission.

In addition to teaming skills, teachers new to teaming will need exposure to teaming practices. At this stage teachers will need to go beyond just learning about these practices. They will need to be involved in planning which practices will be used and how they will be implemented in their own teaming situations. Much of the material in the rest of this chapter and in subsequent chapters could form the basis for staff development concerning the practice of teaming. Teaming practices include such elements as (1) setting expectations and goals, (2) conducting team meetings, (3) keeping records, (4) tending to students' needs, (5) integrating instruction, and (6) monitoring the development of teaming. These six critical issues will need to be dealt with by the teachers who will form the new teacher teams. Beginning a year before the initial implementation and continuing throughout the first year of teaming, staff development regarding the practice of teaming will be indispensable to the success of team organization.

Setting Expectations and Goals

Teams, like any other type of organization, will go nowhere and become a source of frustration if their members do not have a sense of direction. Two of the earlier tasks that teams need to accomplish are (1) to determine members' expectations of each other and of the team as a unit and (2) to set some goals to focus the efforts of the team. The term *expectations* refers to decisions about how communication will occur within the team, how decisions will be made, how various housekeeping chores will be taken care of, and how communication with people outside of the team will be conducted. In other words, expectations are some of the nitty-gritty issues that need conscious consideration in order to avoid future conflicts over "little matters." On the other hand, *goals* are statements related to the mission of the team. They can be short-term, relating to things the team would like to accomplish during the current semester, or they can be long-term, relating to what the team envisions itself accomplishing after one or two years of development (more on the issue of development in the next section). Short-term goals are particularly important for new teams because they provide a bench mark against which to assess their progress in the short run.

31

However, before individual teams can productively discuss their expectations and goals, some decisions need to be made at the district level and at the building level regarding the role of teams in the larger school context. Since teams are a subsystem of larger units—the school and the district—team-level planning must be done in the context of these larger units. If a school district creates teams just because they are a "good idea" or the "latest educational advancement," without setting out guidelines for how these teams should operate and relate to the larger school setting, then confusion and wasted effort will result. On the other hand, administrators must guard against overprescribing the procedures that will govern the operation of the teams. It is possible to provide so much outside direction to the teams that they are enervated rather than energized. The district's guidelines for team operation should be stated broadly enough to allow individual teams to make their own decisions within the guidelines set for them. For example, it would be perfectly appropriate for the district to insist that teams determine and write down their own sets of goals for the semester. However, a systemwide set of goals should not be written for all teams in the district. In the next section we will explain further why this practice should be avoided. As a second example of this issue, it is appropriate to stipulate at the district level that all teams must keep written agendas and records of their meetings. Yet individual teams should be given some leeway regarding how they will form agendas and how they will keep their own records. There must be clearly communicated guidelines regarding the work of the teams. With these guidelines in place, teams can then proceed to make team-level decisions concerning the expectations that they have for the operation of *their own* teams in addition to the substantive goals that they will jointly attempt to accomplish.

Goal setting is clearly a multilevel undertaking. Teams cannot write useful goals for themselves if it hasn't been made clear at the district level what it is expected that teaming will accomplish. These district-level expectations will probably vary from year to year as teams mature and as the district's needs change. Team-level goal setting should always take place within the parameters established by district-level and school-level authorities. How can these authorities be helped to establish their expectations for teaming? We turn to that question in the next section.

Setting a Time Line for Evolving Teams

As Hall and others (38, 39, 41) have described, education innovations do not just appear full-blown on the scene. Team organization is no different. In fact, instituting teams may well be one of the more profound changes that will ever be made in a school. For that reason it is very important to plan for the gradual implementation of teaching teams. What is reasonable to expect of teams in the first semester of operation is quite different from what is reasonable to expect in the second or third year of teaming. It is certainly different from high hopes held out for team organization in the areas of interdisciplinary curriculum coordination and joint instructional planning, which are often cited as reasons for going to teaming. As mentioned earlier, specific teams will evolve in different ways and at different paces. Several attempts have been made to describe this aspect of teaming.

George (29) identified four phases in the development of interdisciplinary teams. The first phase is one of "organization" during which teachers begin to function together within the basic organizational features of teaming that were described in Chapter 1. George called phase two "community." During this phase, team members engage in conscious behavior to promote a sense of community among the teachers, students, and parents who make up a team. It is not until phase three that the team enters the "team teaching" level of development. This phase requires time, interest, and skill that is often not yet present in the first two phases. Finally, evolving teams may reach the "governmental" phase. This phase can be reached as it becomes clear to both teachers and administrators that teachers working together on teams can share decision-making power with the principal for the improved management of the school building. Certain things have to happen at each lower phase in order for the team to attain the prerequisites to move on to a higher phase. A sense of community cannot develop until teachers begin working together under conditions in which they share students and a common meeting time. Teachers cannot coordinate curriculum and integrate instruction until they have had enough time to build a sense of mutual trust, learn about each other's curricular areas, and develop the skills of collaboration.

Pickler (63) provided a five-stage description of team evolution based on his observations. In his system the stages represent an evolution "from strictly organizational functions to team climate/ identity concerns and on to instructional applications" (p. 6). Garvin (28) described what he calls "reasonable levels of interdisciplinary teaming" (Figure 2.7). He provided a three-year list of expectations for teams. Because teams do evolve at different rates, administrators are faced with the problem of setting basic expectations for all teams without at the same time holding back or stifling teams that are ready to do more sophisticated things.

Figure 2.7

Reasonable Levels of Interdisciplinary Teaming

LEVEL I—FIRST-YEAR EXPECTATIONS:

Coordination of homework
Coordination of testing
Establish workable policies on discipline
Parent conferencing
Adopt a Team project

LEVEL II—SECOND-YEAR EXPECTATIONS

Work at changing group sizes
Rotating schedules
Meet more regularly with specialist
Brainstorm interdisciplinary units
Visit students in related arts
Cooperative field trips
Brainstorm alternative grouping possibilities

LEVEL III—MAY BEGIN BEFORE THE THIRD YEAR BUT NOT SO IN MANY CASES

Share teaching objectives
Make curriculum developmental
Team teaching
Other:
        Skill days

Source: Reprinted with permission of the National Middle School Association from a handout distributed in conjunction with the presentation of "A Positive Approach to Interdisciplinary Team Organization" by James P. Garvin at the 1987 NMSA annual meeting, St. Louis.

Recognizing that they would be supervising teams at several levels of development, yet wanting to establish the minimum level of functioning expected, the principals in the Shawnee Mission (Kansas) Public Schools created a multiyear, multilevel planning grid (Figure 2.8). These principals were faced with the need to provide guidance and coordination for twenty to thirty teaching teams operating in seven separate middle schools districtwide. Across the bottom row the principals established the basic expectations for all teams for a three-year period. In this row the principals set forth the nonnegotiable minimum criteria regarding meeting times, record keeping, goal setting, professional growth, and student grouping. For the first year, in the "Desired" row the principals listed those things that they hoped would occur on most teams beyond the basics. These expectations related to communication with school support staff, communication with parents, development of team identity, and coordinated planning to meet students' academic needs. Recognizing that some teams were composed of people who had worked together before or who had experience on pilot teams, the principals laid out in the "Optimum" row some things that they expected to occur in the most advanced teams during the first year. Such expectations included use of themes and mascots to promote self-identity, communication with exploratory and elective area teachers concerning students and curricular coordination, and skill integration across the various subject areas taught on the team. For each succeeding year the expectations for basic, desired, and optimal functioning of teams were raised. The principals would not expect interdisciplinary thematic units planned to fully integrate the curriculum and skills taught in the various subject areas until the third year of operation at the optimal level. The use of such a grid allows those responsible for managing the operation of teams to provide direction for these teams at the district level while at the same time allowing for individuality in the development of different teams. It also helps administrators resist the temptation to overplan and overprescribe for the operation of teams. Basic expectations are clarified. However, the basics do not become a ceiling that holds back teams wishing to move forward at a faster pace.

Although no two teams evolve in exactly the same way, a fairly consistent pattern of stages has emerged from the attempts to characterize the development of teams: (1) settling issues related to

Figure 2.8 Long-Range Planning

	Year 1	Year 2	Year 3
OPTIMUM	• Team themes and mascots • Communicate with exploratory and elective teachers • Skill integration		• Integrate curriculum and skills including materials from the exploration program • Plan integrated units of study
DESIRED	• Scheduled contact with support personnel • Increased parent communication • Development of team identity • Planning to meet student academic needs		
EXPECTATIONS	• Meet daily • Keep records including an agenda, minutes, and parent contact log • Develop team goals and expectations for the team and for students • Actively, positively participate • Do joint planning that provides for the academic, social, emotional, and physical needs of students • Be self-directive in team organization to include the use of a plan for professional growth and development • Group students for instruction including the flexible use of time		

Source: Developed by the Shawnee Mission (Kansas) Public Schools. Reprinted with permission.

meetings and management, (2) addressing student needs, (3) promoting personal professional growth and collective responsibility, and (4) coordinating curriculum and integrating instruction. The issues discussed in this chapter and the next—determining roles, setting agendas, keeping records, setting procedures for communicating with support staff, and building a team schedule—receive emphasis in the category of things to do "very early" in the development of teaming. However, before the first year is concluded, teachers tend to turn their attention to issues related to meeting the needs of students on their teams. Such issues as discussing students in need, developing joint plans of action to deal with the identified needs, communicating with appropriate support staff (e.g., counselors, special educators, social workers, nurses), and planning and carrying out parent conferences come to the fore. Once teachers have worked out most of the management issues and satisfied themselves that they are doing a better job of meeting the needs of their students, they turn their attention to their own professional growth and to the collective well-being of the team. Use of the team structure for developing staff, sharing ideas about instruction, discovering ways to coordinate the curriculum, promoting the *"we* can do" spirit, and further involving students in decision making concerning the life of the team receives greater emphasis in the second or third year that teams function together. Finally, some teams that have successfully solved the management questions, made good progress on meeting the needs of students, and developed strong professional bonds are ready to function at the very highest level expected of team organization. Seeing themselves as jointly responsible for the basic instruction of a group of students, these teachers plan together to use the block schedule flexibly to teach a number of interdisciplinary thematic units that reinforce not only skills but also understandings across subject matters. Students are then grouped and regrouped frequently in response to the requirements of a variety of learning activities and of various student characteristics. (The issue of instruction on teams will be dealt with more thoroughly in Chapter 4.)

The sequence of stages that we have just described must not be thought of as a rigid lock-step model of team development. Each stage represents a set of emphases or priorities that require most of the team's energy. For example, while settling management issues will necessarily dominate the deliberations of a team in the early

37

stages of its development, such issues will never completely go away. Questions related to conducting team meetings, communicating with support staff, and designing forms for carrying out the work of the team will continue to come up from time to time. However, these issues will no longer dominate the time and energy of the team. Once these issues are determined, the energy of the team turns naturally to meeting student needs. Likewise, later in the evolution of the team when it is using much of its energy to develop interdisciplinary units, the need to discuss and make decisions regarding meeting student needs will not go away. However, by this time the team will have become more efficient in dealing with student needs so that more of its energy can be devoted to interdisciplinary planning. Furthermore, by this time the team will be seeing ways to integrate its interdisciplinary planning into the meeting of student needs. In effect, as teams evolve into higher levels of functioning, they incorporate elements of the previous stages of decision making into each new higher level.

MERGING WITH THE SCHOOL AT LARGE

When setting up interdisciplinary teams for the first time, a faculty needs to consider the relationships among the newly organized teams and other elements of the school organization, such as special education, the guidance program, other teachers not on basic subjects teams, academic departments, school leadership, and other teams. Though the relationships between and among these various elements will evolve over time, just as the teams themselves will evolve internally, some thought must be given at the onset of teaming to the initial relationships that will exist.

Special Education

Examining the relationship between teams and special education brings up the larger issue of assigning students to teams. As much as possible each team in the school should represent a microcosm of the whole school. Teams should be balanced according to gender, ethnicity, socioeconomic background, and student ability. Failure to do so will inevitably have a negative impact on school climate. If one team gets identified as the "gifted" team and another one the "special education" team and another one the

38

"problem student" team, a whole host of negative results can be anticipated. Parents will badger the principal to have their children assigned to the "good" team. Student self-esteem will be negatively affected. Teacher morale will plummet as teachers vie to be assigned to the best teams and avoid the undesirable ones. By far the best practice for assigning students to teams is to seek balance of those factors relevant to the local setting. However, occasionally in the "real world" it becomes necessary to place all band students or whomever on a single team. When this occurs, those responsible for scheduling students onto teams need to look for other ways to keep the teams balanced so that one of them does not come to be perceived as the "smart" team and another one the "dumb" team. It goes without saying that schools small enough to have only one team per grade level will escape this dilemma since all students at that grade level will be assigned to the same team.

The issue of assigning students to teams has particular relevance when it comes to placing mainstreamed special education students on regular education interdisciplinary teams. On the one hand, you do not want one team to be perceived as the "learning disabled" or the "emotionally disturbed" team. On the other hand, you do not want to create impossible communications barriers between special educators and regular educators by spreading an LD teacher's students among six different teams. Since one of the advantages of team organization is that special educators can meet regularly with team teachers during their common planning time, creating a situation in which a given special education teacher would have to meet with six different teams is not a good idea. The specific solution to this dilemma will depend on a number of local factors, such as the number of special education students in the several categories being assigned to teams, the number of special education teachers assigned to the building, and the communications network among the special education teachers themselves. Kerble (49) described the solution to this dilemma that was adopted at the Higgins Middle School in Peabody, Massachusetts. If the special education program is large enough, perhaps different special education teachers can be assigned to different teams so that any one of them would have to conference with only one or two teams. With a large number of mainstreamed students to spread around, balance might easily be achieved on the teams. In situations where the special education program is relatively small, it might make sense to concentrate all special students on one or two teams to ensure that special and regular educators have access to one another. When this occurs, the balancing of student ability levels may have to be accomplished in other ways—for example, by making sure students at the other end of the ability scale are not concentrated on another team.

In any case the key to promoting successful mainstreaming in a school with team organization is to balance the student membership on the teams against the need to promote open, face-to-face, frequent communication among special and regular educators. Where this balance has been properly struck, special educators have become valued members of interdisciplinary teams. They often come to act as resource teachers to the team, offering counsel concerning the learning needs of many different types of students. When this has occurred, special educators and regular educators have come to regard *all* the students on a team as "*our* students." Gone are the attitudes revealed in the expressions "my students" and "their students" that have been used, for example, to distinguish between "my English students" and "their emotionally disturbed students"! Since interdisciplinary teams will very likely be functioning in schools where special education programs are already in existence, careful thought needs to be given as to how these two elements will work together for the benefit of students.

The Guidance Program

At the time teams are established, some type of guidance program is usually already in existence. Or perhaps, as in the case of junior high to middle school conversions, major changes may be occurring simultaneously in the guidance program through the implementation of an advisory program. Team organization can have a profound effect on the functioning of the guidance program by altering the way in which counselors do their jobs and by integrating what teachers do in team meetings with what counselors do with advisees in the advisory program.

One of the biggest changes that will occur with the implementation of team organization is the creation of the opportunity for the counselor(s) to meet regularly with four or five teachers who all know a specific student. In a departmentalized school when the case of "Johnny Jones" comes to the attention of his counselor,

40

the counselor has to find a way to track down each of Johnny's teachers individually, often resorting to passing notes via mailboxes, in order to get an overview of how Johnny is doing in his classes. In a team situation the counselor may have first learned of Johnny's problems from his teachers in a face-to-face meeting. When setting up new teams, arrangements need to be made to schedule the counselor(s) into team meetings on a regular basis. In large schools, which have two or more counselors available, thought must be given as to how students will be assigned to these counselors. In departmentalized schools it may be all right to alphabetically assign students to counselors. However, in a teamed setting if students are assigned alphabetically to counselors, each counselor may have to meet with every team in order to discuss students' needs. This will lead to very inefficient use of time for both teachers and counselors. Therefore, in a teamed setting students need to be assigned to counselors by team. Consequently, when Counselor Smith sits down with Team B, every student to be discussed is shared by both the counselor and the teamed teachers. More will be said on teacher-counselor interaction in Chapter 3.

When looking for ways to integrate the advisory program with team organization, there is no one best way to proceed. However, several factors need to be considered in planning how these two elements will work together. An advisory program (43) is built around the idea that in a school setting where students interact with several subject area teachers, there should be one adult who knows each child as a person and who assumes responsibility for seeing to it that that child gets the academic and moral support he or she needs to succeed in school. Typically the advisee-to-advisor ratio is between 15:1 and 25:1, meaning that an advisory group is formed by assigning one adult to every fifteen to twenty-five students. One of the advisor's chief duties is to keep an up-to-date overview of how each advisee is doing in the total school setting, which is typically fragmented for the student by interactions with different teachers. It begins to become clear that the team meeting, during which student needs are discussed by four or five teachers who know the student, is a convenient vehicle for gaining a broad overview of how well a student is doing in several different classrooms. Therefore, it may make sense to assign advisors to students on a team-by-team basis. This practice facilitates advisors' efforts to keep up to date with regard to their advisees. However, using only the interdisciplinary team teachers would exclude other teachers from being advisors and result in rather large advisory groups. Consequently, an interdisciplinary team is often expanded into an "advisory" team by adding two or three other teachers to the basic team for the purpose of facilitating the advisory program in which students are assigned to advisory groups by teams. Assigning students to interdisciplinary teams, to counselors, and to advisory groups in a coordinated fashion can reinforce the work of each element in the service of students.

Other Teachers

Assigning some teachers to interdisciplinary teams raises the question of the relationship between these teachers on teams and the other teachers, such as the industrial education, art, music, physical education, and computer science teachers, who also teach the same students. In departmentalized schools the issue is seldom raised to a conscious level because coordination across departments is not even considered a possibility. But with the advent of team organization, educators can conceive of new possibilities. In some cases these other teachers, often referred to as *exploratory* or *elective subject teachers*, are themselves organized onto modified interdisciplinary teams of their own. These teams are modified in the sense that although these teachers share common planning time on a regular basis, they may not share the same students at any one time because of the way the elective/exploratory schedule is set up. Very seldom do elective or exploratory teachers share common space because of the quite different requirements of an industrial arts classroom, a physical education classroom, an art room, and a music room. A block schedule is seldom part of the picture, although some schools manage to schedule an arts block or an exploration block. However, the elective specialists do share some common problems and need the access to the building administration that can occur during their team meetings.

The most fundamental question that will arise with the onset of teaming is how the basic interdisciplinary team teachers will communicate with the elective/exploratory teachers regarding students' needs. When the teamed teachers identify "Susie Smith" as a student who is having difficulty in her basic classes, how will these teachers involve the rest of Susie's teachers in discussing and devising a joint solution to Susie's problem? Once again there is no one right way to deal with this dilemma, a dilemma exacerbated by the almost universal condition that when the teamed teachers are meeting, elective teachers are teaching and are not readily available to attend a meeting to discuss Susie's problem.

Several strategies have been used in an effort to overcome this predicament. In one school the teamed teachers in a moment of whimsy created their "adopt a wild child" program. Each team member "adopted" an exploratory/elective teacher to keep in touch with on an as-needed basis. Since every teamed teacher had an individual planning period in addition to the team meeting time, each team teacher would be paired with an elective teacher who shared that individual planning period. As a result, if either the team teacher or the elective teacher felt that a student's needs should be discussed in a team meeting, she or he could convey that belief to the other party. When the case of Susie Smith is to be discussed during the team meeting, input from the concerned elective teachers could be gathered in several different ways. First, the elective teachers might provide a short written note for use in the meeting and then receive a short written summary of the outcome of the meeting. In other cases a team teacher or an administrator could cover the elective teacher's class for a few minutes, freeing that elective teacher to participate personally in the discussion of Susie's problem. These same strategies could be used if a subsequent conference were to be set up with Susie's parents. Teaming increases the amount of conversation in a school concerning students' needs, and elective and exploratory teachers can come to feel left out of this discussion if plans are not made to involve them from the beginning.

Another issue that can arise, but usually not at the onset of teaming, is how to involve elective and exploratory teachers in interdisciplinary thematic units. As we noted before, the planning of such units will probably not occur within the interdisciplinary team until two or three years have passed. But at some point, when it becomes clear that the teamed teachers can plan for the integration of their subjects through interdisciplinary units, the elective teachers will probably want in on the action. As the teams evolve, it may well become necessary to think about how some all-school or at least all-grade-level units can be planned that will tie together English, art, mathematics, social studies, physical education, science, and music. Several such units have been implemented successfully and can provide ideas that can be accomplished in your setting. Chapter 5 contains an annotated bibliography of some successful interdisciplinary units.

Academic Departments

Because team organization is often favorably compared to departmentalized organization, confusion frequently occurs as to whether the two concepts can coexist in the same building. The idea that teaming must abide at the expense of departmentalization is only partially true. Indeed, departments in a school with teaching teams do not fulfill the same roles that they do when they are the major organizing feature for the faculty. However, academic departments do retain important functions in schools with team organization. While teams are very good for organizing the day-to-day instruction of students assigned to them, teams alone are not set up to coordinate the curriculum across grade levels or even across teams at the same grade level. Academic departments need to continue to coordinate the various parts of the curriculum from year to year and to articulate the curriculum with schools at other levels in the K–12 program. Often the management of supply budgets to support the various curricular areas remains a function of the departments. However, in the development and maintenance of curriculum, the departments no longer function in isolation from each other when they coexist with teams. Indeed, the opportunities for integrating instruction across subject areas that teaming provides should influence departmental curriculum planners when they revise curricula and select support materials.

Building Administration

As demonstrated in Chapter 1, teachers' access to building-level decision making will be altered in a teamed setting. Though we will elaborate much more on how this happens in the next chapter, it is important to remind ourselves at this point that communications patterns with administrators will change when principals have the opportunity to sit down with small groups of four or five teachers on a regular basis. Issues can be discussed much more effectively than they usually are when the whole faculty assembles for a four o'clock meeting on Tuesday afternoon. New and creative ideas have a greater chance of being articulated when smaller numbers of people can sit down and talk them out. Some principals choose to work through team leaders to keep in touch with what is happening on teams. The team leader's role as a representative of team views to the principal and as a representative of the principal's views to the team teachers is enlarged when a principal chooses to operate in this way. Whichever way the principal functions, teachers and administrators tend to have greater access to each other's thinking if teachers are organized in teams.

Other Teams

As with departments, teams exist not alone but in conjunction with other teams at different grade levels, at the same grade level, at multiple grade levels, and/or in the exploratory/elective areas. If careful planning does not occur when team organization is being designed, one might hear teachers lament: "I have no idea what the social studies teacher on the other seventh grade team is doing," or "We would like to know what last year's team did with our students." Part of the answer to these laments is to be found in the maintenance of curricular departments as discussed above. However, the issue of cross-team communication cannot be solved by departments alone. One of the most important roles of the grade-level coordinator, teaming project coordinator, or team coordinator is to act as a little bumblebee cross-pollinating ideas among teams. Not only is curricular information conveyed from team to team by the team coordinator, but also ideas related to classroom management, student discipline, instructional strategies, and the management of team business get distributed this way.

SUMMARY

The extent and breadth of this chapter should help to reinforce the idea that staff development for the successful implementation of teams must begin during the academic year prior to that in which teams are actually formed. There is so much that must be thought out and planned for if teams are to get off to a relatively smooth start. Teaming requires more than just the scheduling of common meeting time and shared students. The people who are going to carry out the work of the teams must decide how they will select team membership, define team roles, set expectations and goals, plan for the gradual implementation of the possibilities, and coordinate teams with the other elements of the school program.

Chapter 3

FACE TO FACE IN TEAMS

DEALING WITH EACH OTHER

In one introductory in-service workshop on teaming, a teacher participant expressed her sentiments about teaming in this way: "The notion of teaming doesn't worry me, but I'd like to know with whom I am going to team?" This single example captures the sentiments of the majority of teachers who face the opportunity of teaming.

While teaming enables teachers to collaborate and communicate in ways that add strength and support to the teaching experience, few would argue that teamwork is without conflict. The inevitable personality differences inherent in any group of two, three, four, or five teachers present one of the more challenging facets of teaming. No doubt some teams literally fall in love immediately, finding among their teammates kindred professional friendship, and this is a wonderful and usually quite serendipitous happening. Likewise, it is possible, as we explained in Chapter 2, to avoid serious personality conflicts by using various prestaffing measures that attempt to take into account extremely sensitive relationships. Nonetheless, the team reality for most teachers begins with at least some measure of discomfort as individuals struggle to merge rather distinct personal and professional world views. So when teachers are face to face in teams, what can be done to facilitate comfortable internal team relations, effective team decision making, and productive teamwork?

The deliberate and careful use of a personality measure in team staffing, as discussed in Chapter 2, can indeed work to prevent major conflicts among teammates. It will not, however, ensure that significant personality differences will not exist on a team. In fact, from our working knowledge of effective teams and from research on effective groups, we have learned that some blend of distinctively difficult personalities is desirable. Blending those differences constructively is a challenge for every working team.

To build effective team relations, it is extremely helpful for teams to acknowledge team members' strengths, interests, personal and professional goals, and basic personality orientations. While formal instruments are helpful, a simple, five-question assessment might enable teams to understand how individual team members approach team problem solving and decision making. Each team member should openly share his or her responses to the following items:

1. When working in groups, I usually organize, structure, and order teamwork.

   _____ Yes   _____ No

2. As a group member, my main interest is in maintaining group harmony and happiness.

   _____ Yes   _____ No

3. When I work in groups, I very often pursue a goal or complete a task single-mindedly, and I prefer to work alone.

   _____ Yes   _____ No

4. I enjoy solving problems and generating creative solutions. My strengths are in creativity, not organization.

   _____ Yes   _____ No

5. In groups, I prefer to work on the details and avoid the idea-generating stage of decision making.

   _____ Yes   _____ No

Responses to these five statements will not yield research-validated personality data. They will provide teams with information useful in discussing personal orientation to teamwork. Complete the five items yourself, and then consider the following typical conflict scenarios:

a. In planning a field day, the social studies teacher has a dozen good ideas with lots of suggestions for each. It seems to her that the science teacher, however, is more interested in getting anything started and tries to hurry the process. The science teacher, on the other hand, dreads the team's brainstorming sessions because they seem to take so long. "How many ideas do we need?" he might ask.

b. It seems to the language arts teacher that both the mathematics and the science teachers often solve problems before concerns and feelings are fully aired. Moreover, she finds that the tension created between the mathematics and the social studies teachers is quite uncomfortable at times.

c. The language arts teacher wants to keep the team happy and suggests an afternoon social before a holiday. The mathematics and the science teachers don't see the point of such social gatherings. There is no animosity here—just disinterest.

In each example of conflict, some degree of resolution might be achieved with reference to personality orientations. In this case it is obvious that the divergent style of the social studies teacher is a source of conflict with that of the science teacher who seeks a single-line approach. However, it should be seen that this divergence is, at the same time, a strength for the team as a whole. Both the social studies teacher and the science teacher bring useful perspectives that help balance problem-solving discussion on the team. Continue with this analysis and it becomes clear that developing an awareness of teammates' individual strengths and styles helps to overcome potential sources of conflict by promoting an appreciation of how divergent viewpoints can make the work of the team more effective.

In addition, it is wise to have an initial team meeting at which team members share their personal skills, strengths, talents, and quirks so the team members can begin to explore just how they will merge and to anticipate just how they might conflict. To approach this process, it might be helpful to have your team members complete the checklist appearing in Figure 3.1, entitled "DOs and DON'Ts," and share their results in some way. While this may seem unnecessary at first glance, teams need to formalize the reflection process in order to establish openness as a group norm and to ensure that all members' sentiments are voiced.

One final initiation exercise helpful in merging team personalities involves a discussion of professional perspectives, practices, and goals. Even among teachers who may have taught in the same building for years, it should not be taken for granted that they know each other's views on these matters. Once again, without

Figure 3.1

DOs and DON'Ts

In any team, there are informal "DOs and DON'Ts." They are rarely written down anywhere, but they serve as a kind of code, making it clear what people in the team should and should not do if they are to be accepted by others.

Below there is a list of specific things that a team member might do or say. We would like to estimate what most people in this team would feel about each item. That is, we want you to tell us whether the predominant feeling of most of the people in this team is that one should or should not do or say the thing in question. You can indicate your answer by placing a check mark (✔) in the appropriate column—Should or Should Not—beside each item.

For example:

I believe that the *majority* of people would feel that you...

	Should	Should Not
X. Follow administrative directives.	✔	
Y. Complain when things are not going right.		✔
Z. Spread rumors.		✔

The above examples would show that you believe most people feel that one should follow administrative directives and that one should neither complain when things are not going right nor spread rumors.

	Should	Should Not
1. Ask others who seem upset to express their feelings directly.		
2. Tell colleagues what you really think of their work.		
3. Look for ulterior motives in other people's behavior.		
4. Always ask "Why?" when you don't know.		
5. Avoid disagreement and conflict whenever possible.		
6. Consult with people under you in making decisions that affect them—even minor ones.		

Source: Adapted with permission from *Diagnosing Professional Climates of Schools* by Robert Fox, Richard Schmuck, Elmer Van Egmond, Miriam Ritvo, and Charles Jung. Copyright 1973, NTL Institute (Learning Resources Corp.).

Figure 3.1 (Continued)

7. Question well-established ways of doing things. ⎯⎯⎯ ⎯⎯⎯

8. Be concerned about other people's problems. ⎯⎯⎯ ⎯⎯⎯

9. Only make a decision after everyone's ideas have been fully heard. ⎯⎯⎯ ⎯⎯⎯

10. Disagree with your superior if you happen to know more about the issue than he or she does. ⎯⎯⎯ ⎯⎯⎯

11. Withhold personal feelings and stick to the logical merits of the case in any discussion. ⎯⎯⎯ ⎯⎯⎯

12. Push for new ideas, even if they are vague or unusual. ⎯⎯⎯ ⎯⎯⎯

13. Ask others to tell you what they really think of your work. ⎯⎯⎯ ⎯⎯⎯

14. Keep your real thoughts and reactions to yourself, by and large. ⎯⎯⎯ ⎯⎯⎯

15. Trust others not to take advantage of you. ⎯⎯⎯ ⎯⎯⎯

16. Be skeptical about things. ⎯⎯⎯ ⎯⎯⎯

17. Point out other people's mistakes to improve working effectiveness. ⎯⎯⎯ ⎯⎯⎯

18. Listen to others' ideas but reserve the decision to yourself. ⎯⎯⎯ ⎯⎯⎯

19. Try out new ways of doing things, even if it's uncertain how they will work out. ⎯⎯⎯ ⎯⎯⎯

20. Stay "cool"—keep your distance from others. ⎯⎯⎯ ⎯⎯⎯

21. Use formal voting as a way of making decisions in small groups. ⎯⎯⎯ ⎯⎯⎯

22. Set up committees that bypass or cut across usual channels or lines of authority. ⎯⎯⎯ ⎯⎯⎯

23. Spend time in meetings on emotional matters not strictly germane to the task. ⎯⎯⎯ ⎯⎯⎯

24. Be critical of unusual or "way out" ideas. ⎯⎯⎯ ⎯⎯⎯

25. Tell other people what they want to hear rather than what you really think. ⎯⎯⎯ ⎯⎯⎯

26. Stick with familiar ways of doing things in one's work. ⎯⎯⎯ ⎯⎯⎯

27. Trust others to help in difficult situations. ⎯⎯⎯ ⎯⎯⎯

some formal structure to encourage this sharing process, teams often overlook this fundamental of team building. Consider using the following questions and suggestions to guide such a meeting:

1. What are three specific educational goals you have for this school year?
2. Share three of your favorite teaching ideas.
3. Describe three instructional principles that guide your teaching practice.
4. In what ways can the team be of help to you as a teacher?

Using this structure enables the team members to open otherwise closed doors to essential understandings. It further invites the educational exchange necessary for productive teamwork.

THE TEAM MEETING:
THE FOUNDATION FOR SUCCESS

Knowing each other, while exceedingly important, does not guarantee effective communication or productive team meetings. A significant number of teams grow distant and unhappy because their communication is wrought with misunderstandings and hurts. Establishing interpersonal understandings for teamwork is indeed a preventive measure, but more needs to be said about basic techniques that are useful in promoting the effective use of team planning time.

Clarifying Team Expectations

Discussing expectations for the operation of the teams is something that might be overlooked in the haste to get going with the headline tasks of teaming (e.g., interdisciplinary teaching, cross-curricular subject matter coordination, group problem solving to meet students' needs, and coordination of the block schedule). However, time spent discussing some rather unsexy management issues very early in the development of teaming is time well spent.

Chief among these issues is the question "How will we conduct our team meetings?" Figure 3.2 contains one team's answer. In August, before they began their first year of teaming, this eighth grade interdisciplinary team *wrote down* its own set of expectations for conducting team meetings.

Figure 3.2

Team Guidelines

1. No absenteeism—unless an emergency.
2. Consensus.
3. Cooperation, openness, honesty, trust, and support.
4. Flexibility.
5. Administration and team leaders settle differences.
6. There will be an agenda and record keeping.
7. Meeting places—lounges, 216, counselor's conference room.
8. Stay on task.
9. Be on time.
10. If guidelines are not followed, the leader will talk to the team member privately, and if the problem continues, the leader will go to the administration.
11. A substitute will sit in on team meetings and participate.
12. Team members should not take decisions personally.
13. If team members are upset, they should air their feelings or tell someone on the team.

Note: These guidelines were developed at the beginning of the *first* year of team organization.

Source: Developed by Hocker Grove Middle School, Shawnee Mission, Kansas. Reprinted with permission.

Teams also need to discuss these additional questions very early in the teaming process:

1. How will items get on an agenda?
2. What should be recorded in the minutes?
3. Who will do the recording?
4. How will we reach decisions?
5. How should we manage communication with others?
6. How will we manage to compile a team calendar?

Setting Team Priorities

In Chapter 2 we looked at the process by which teams evolve and at how administrators can manage the complexity of teams evolving at different rates. We then examined the changing emphases that emerge as teams anticipate their development from collections of individual teachers thrown together by the circumstances of common schedules, common space, and shared students into true organic units functioning in an integrated fashion. The question that we now face is how teams themselves can be helped to manage this development at the individual team level. In this section we will provide an exercise that teachers have used to discuss and set team priorities.

When teams are formed for the first time, their members are faced with the problem of how to use the new resources of time and space that have been made available to them. A useful first step is for team members to brainstorm a list of things that they can do with colleagues, with students, and with subject matter that cannot be done as well, or at all, in a departmentalized organization with a rigid bell schedule. It is not uncommon for teachers to generate lists of thirty or more items! As the potential of teaming becomes clearer for teachers, the panic of deciding where to begin sets in.

The Aurora (Colorado) Public Schools use a decision-making document called the Build-a-Team Spectrum to help team teachers set priorities among all the possibilities for teaming. An adapted and expanded version of this document appears in Figure 3.3. It allows teachers to analyze forty possible team activities, all of which are currently being done by teams at various levels of development. Each team must decide for itself what is reasonable to undertake at its current level of development. By grouping the possibilities into (1) those things that are reasonable to do *very early* in the development of teaming, (2) those things that are reasonable to do *later* during the *first year* of teaming, (3) those things that are reasonable to do during the *second or third year* of teaming, and (4) those things that are reasonable to do only in the *latest or most advanced stages* of teaming, teachers can begin to comprehend the developmental process as it applies to their own situation.

The Agenda

Given that achieving effective team meetings is a top priority, how should teams proceed? Are there some secrets for success? Erring on the side of being too casual is the first trap to avoid. Comfortable and casual are not synonymous. Second, teams might

Figure 3.3

So Many Possibilities. . .Only So Much Time: Setting Team Priorities

Group these possible activities into one of four categories:

A. Reasonable to do *very early* in the development of teaming

B. Reasonable to do *later* during the *first year*

C. Reasonable in the *second or third year*

D. Reasonable only in the *latest* or *most advanced stages* of team development.

_____ 1. Schedule students *within* the team's block of time.

_____ 2. Meet regularly.

_____ 3. Set consistent expectations for team members (teachers).

_____ 4. Rotate team leader position so that each member has an opportunity.

_____ 5. Share major curriculum thrusts with team members.

_____ 6. Develop a team process for recognizing students who are doing well.

_____ 7. Build a team schedule for homework and testing.

_____ 8. Determine important skills for the team (e.g., note taking, notebook organization, listening skills) and consistently include them in all classes.

_____ 9. Determine activities that could be delivered in a large group setting (e.g., showing films, testing, listening to outside speakers) and implement them.

_____10. Teach a unit using community resources in which we share the teaching of activities across subjects.

_____11. Set consistent behavioral expectations for students.

_____12. Discuss a problematic student with the counselor.

_____13. Discuss educational philosophy with team members.

_____14. Discuss needs of individual students.

_____15. Meet together to plan for a conference with parents.

_____16. Conference with students.

_____17. Develop a system of positive consequences and recognition for students.

_____18. Alter the basic schedule to provide for films, videotapes, speakers, labs, etc.

Figure 3.3 (Continued)

___19. Conduct team meetings with students.

___20. Share curriculum plans with the library/media specialist.

___21. Play an active role in school policy making.

___22. Coordinate lessons to reinforce each other's subjects.

___23. Bounce ideas off of team members.

___24. Implement a representative team council to provide for student input.

___25. Share information about students and develop a team solution to problems.

___26. Develop agendas for team meetings.

___27. Plan and implement brief interdisciplinary lessons and units (e.g., graphing, applying the metric system, using reference materials, reading critically) among some team members.

___28. Rotate the team recorder position so each member has an opportunity to keep minutes and records for the team.

___29. Work to build team identity.

___30. Plan and implement one major interdisciplinary unit per year throughout the entire team (teenage problems, courage, energy, exploration, and interdependence are examples of thematic units; information gathering, small group techniques, public speaking, and critical thinking are examples of skill units).

___31. Hold parent conferences as a team.

___32. Share successful teaching experiences with team members.

___33. Plan to reinforce an academic skill across several subject areas.

___34. Phone the parents of a student with academic problems.

___35. Develop a rapport with team members.

___36. Plan an interdisciplinary unit with elective/exploratory teachers.

___37. Share ideas with teammates after attending an out-of-district professional meeting.

___38. Participate as a team in an I.E.P. conference.

___39. Learn about specific students' health problems from the school nurse.

___40. Plan and implement one major interdisciplinary unit per term on the team.

Make a grid and group your responses by category.

Source: Adapted with permission from material developed by the Aurora (Colorado) Public Schools.

examine the following suggested practices, which are designed to promote more effective use of team time.

Effective meetings are guided by an appropriate agenda. Daily agendas may not always be necessary, especially for experienced teams, but weekly agendas are essential for all teams.

- Acquire team agenda items for the next meeting at the close of each meeting.
- Solicit agenda items between meetings, particularly when daily team planning is not possible.
- Solicit agenda items from nonteamed staff (e.g., counselors, media specialists) as needed.
- Include agenda items from the school's steering committee meetings.
- Prepare realistic agendas that are also balanced in focus (e.g., repetitive discussions of at-risk students can become counterproductive).
- Have specific goals or target items for each meeting.
- Open one meeting each week with one or two minutes of round robin sharing to address "joys and concerns."
- Save agendas in a team file.
- Post agendas in the team's planning space.
- Design a form to guide agenda planning and recording. One easy-to-use example is presented in Figure 3.4.

The Division of Labor: Team Roles and Responsibilities

Teams that pay attention to internal management issues usually find themselves to be less frustrated and more productive than teams that do not. In addition to establishing guidelines for team meetings, setting priorities, and organizing agendas, effective teams are usually somewhat systematic in their division of labor. One way of dividing up the work of the team is illustrated by an arrangement derived by an eighth grade team at Westridge Middle School in Shawnee Mission, Kansas (Figure 3.5). This five-person team has designated five roles to be fulfilled. All these roles are rotated among the team members throughout the course of the year.

Figure 3.4

Curriculum Area Team Minutes Form

Coordinator: Team:

Recorder: Date:

       AGENDA   DECISION/OUTCOME

1.

2.

3.

4.

5.

6.

7.

8.

9.

10.

Team Members Present:
Team Members Absent:
Next Scheduled Meeting—Date:_____
                    Place:_____
                    Time:_____

Source: Developed by Hines Middle School, Newport News, Virginia. Reprinted with permission.

In the case of this Westridge Middle School team, the team leader is the person in charge of arranging the team meeting agendas, conducting the meetings, and taking care of external communications with other school personnel and parents. Each member serves as team leader for seven weeks at a time. The other

Figure 3.5

Team Responsibility Rotation

	Week 1	Week 2	Week 3	Week 4
Teacher A	Leader*	Leader	Leader	Leader
Teacher B	Books	Forms	Minutes	Calendar
Teacher C	Calendar	Books	Forms	Minutes
Teacher D	Minutes	Calendar	Books	Forms
Teacher E	Forms	Minutes	˙Calendar	Books

*The leadership role is rotated every seven weeks. The other four roles are rotated weekly.

Source: Adapted with permission from information supplied by Team 8–6 at Westridge Middle School, Shawnee Mission, Kansas.

four roles are rotated weekly. The bookkeeper maintains the team's "Blue Book," which contains information sheets on each student on the team. The Blue Book also contains faculty newsletters, school newsletters, records of parent conferences, and team-generated material, such as descriptions of curriculum that are used for parents' back-to-school night. The bookkeeper keeps these student sheets and other records current. The people who fulfill the other three roles also file the products of their labor in the Blue Book. One person is responsible for the team calendar, which contains upcoming special events as well as scheduled tests and major projects. The person responsible for the minutes keeps a record of the decisions that the team makes during its meetings. These are recorded on lined NCR paper so that the special education teacher and other nonteam staff can receive a copy of the minutes, while the team files the original in its Blue Book. The person in charge of forms is responsible for seeing to it that the team has all the forms necessary to carry out its work. These include everything from student progress reports to change-of-class forms for students.

In addition, teams should be cautioned not to exclude duties that attend to the affective side of team life, such as:

1. A timekeeper to watch the clock and facilitate team on-task behavior

2. A harmony keeper to maintain healthy team interactions (This individual clearly emerges early in the life of a team and usually is a person with humor and without hostility.)

3. A climate tender to promote the positive.

Team Decision Making

There are numerous models or paradigms for effective group decision making. Almost all include six basic steps. We suggest that teams affirm and adopt some simple step-by-step formula for team decision making. With each problem to be solved, teams should generally do the following:

Step 1:   Define the problem clearly

Step 2:   Brainstorm action alternatives

Step 3:   Critique each alternative

Step 4:   Select a plan of action

Step 5:   Implement the plan

Step 6:   Evaluate and follow up

Some additional clarification of this process is provided in the following seven steps:

1. Prepare for the meeting.

   a.   Have a clear idea of why you are meeting.

   b.   Prepare the agenda in advance.

   c.   Assemble the materials needed.

   d.   Block off the time needed for the meeting.

2. Adopt a plan for managing the meeting. There are five elements without which a meeting does not run smoothly.

   a.   Start and stop at agreed times.

   b.   Agree on the agenda.

   c.   Hear from everyone who wants to contribute.

   d.   Keep on the topic.

   e.   Keep records during and after the meeting.

3. Analyze the problem.

   a. Study the situation and state the facts.

   b. Examine people's assumptions about the situation.

   c. Consider the boundaries within which the group works.

4. Examine the possibilities for action.

   a. Brainstorm ideas.

   b. Propose tasks or goals.

   c. Consider alternate plans.

   d. Test the consequences of a plan.

5. Decide on an action plan.

   a. Reconsider the problem; clear up any confusion and ambiguity.

   b. Design the plan.

   c. Agree on work assignments.

   d. Agree on a timetable and communication plan.

6. Keep group processes moving. While the group is acting on its agenda and following the problem-solving sequence, some members must be giving attention to the interpersonal processes of the group.

   a. Encourage members' participation and sharing.

   b. Protect members' rights to have their opinions known and feelings aired.

   c. Bridge differences and conflicts between members.

   d. Help the group to be aware of its procedures and interactions and to consider changes if needed.

   e. Clarify, elaborate, and summarize ideas and suggestions; offer conclusions for the group to accept or reject.

   f. Ask for clarification, elaboration, or summary.

   g. Ask for expression of feelings and concerns.

   h. Try to ensure that everyone shares in the decisions being made.

   i. Be constantly alert to what the group process needs at any moment to move it ahead.

7. Carry out the meeting's decisions and plans.

a. Refrain from altering the plan without the group's consent.

b. Keep complaints for the next meeting.

c. Protect the confidences of the meeting. (31, pp. 139–40)

It might be helpful to have a team chart or checklist available and visible to remind your team of the steps necessary for effective decision making. The steps most frequently shortchanged involve problem analysis and follow-up. These are particularly critical because team discussion must be couched in a thorough understanding of the problem to be addressed.

In addition to these general items of import, teams might note that in some cases it is simply best to postpone decision making. Our advice is to table items if the team sees that elaborate discussion is needed to reach a decision, and there is little time remaining, or if there is such extensive conflict that everyone needs additional time to research and reflect.

Internal Team Evaluation

As small organizations, teams can be less formal about evaluating their own effectiveness than larger ones can be. Nonetheless, it is terribly important that teams set aside time on occasion to evaluate their internal processes, including team meetings. Just the act of evaluation creates a climate of professional integrity vital to team success. Consider the evaluation instrument in Figure 3.6 for its content and focus. It suggests key points to examine in the team meeting evaluation process. Although the frequency of team evaluation can vary from team to team, research shows that a regular reevaluation of the teaming process benefits team effectiveness. At the very least, groups that are new to teaming should evaluate their progress at midyear and again at the end of the school year.

In addition to evaluating the team meeting itself, teams should evaluate other critical internal dynamics. Figure 3.7 contains an instrument that can be used by each team member for personal growth and development. While completed individually, it covers almost exhaustively all aspects of effective team dynamics. Teams could make use of this information in a wide variety of ways to better understand the dynamics of teaming.

Figure 3.6

The Team Meeting Evaluation

	Consistently	Frequently	Occasionally	Seldom

1. Are the goals of the agenda stated realistically?

2. Have the goals of the agenda been achieved?

3. Is team planning time kept strictly for team business?

4. Does everyone participate equally in team decisions?

5. Have team decisions been carried out?

6. Are leadership responsibilities shared?

7. Do students benefit from the team's efforts?

8. What areas need more attention?

_____

_____

_____

_____

Source: Developed by the Orange County Public Schools, Orlando, Florida. Reprinted with permission.

TYPICAL PROBLEMS ENCOUNTERED IN TEAM MEETINGS

Staying on Task

Most teams struggle with the difficulty of divergent dialogue. Staying on task during team meetings is indeed a challenge. Agenda items are often connected to other equally important issues, which can move front and center and divert a team from its agenda. Sometimes these divergences can be crucial to creative problem solving. At other times they can be vital to the team's mental health. However, such wanderings from the agenda often cause frustrations because they lead to meetings that lack focus and closure. If this becomes a team pattern, team productivity is compromised, and some plan of action must be instituted.

Figure 3.7

Goals for Personal Development As Team Member

This form is to help you think about various aspects of your relationships with others and your skills in teamwork. It gives you a chance to set your own goals for development. The steps in using it are:

1. Read through the list and decide which items you are doing all right on, which ones you should do more often, and which ones you should do less often. Mark each item in the appropriate place.

2. Some aspects of group interaction that are not listed may be more important to you than those listed. Write in such aspects on the blank lines.

Communications Skills	Doing all right	Need to do it more	Need to do it less
1. Talking in the group	_____	_____	_____
2. Being brief and concise	_____	_____	_____
3. Being forceful	_____	_____	_____
4. Drawing others out	_____	_____	_____
5. Listening alertly	_____	_____	_____
6. Thinking before I talk	_____	_____	_____
7. Keeping my remarks on the topic	_____	_____	_____
8. _____	_____	_____	_____

Figure 3.7 (Continued)

Observation Skills	Doing all right	Need to do it more	Need to do it less
1. Noting tension in group	_____	_____	_____
2. Noting who talks to whom	_____	_____	_____
3. Noting interest level of group	_____	_____	_____
4. Sensing feelings of individuals	_____	_____	_____
5. Noting who is being "left out"	_____	_____	_____
6. Noting reactions to my comments	_____	_____	_____
7. Noting when group avoids a topic	_____	_____	_____
8. _____	_____	_____	_____

Problem-Solving Skills	Doing all right	Need to do it more	Need to do it less
1. Stating problems or goals	_____	_____	_____
2. Asking for ideas, opinions	_____	_____	_____
3. Giving ideas, opinions	_____	_____	_____
4. Evaluating ideas critically	_____	_____	_____
5. Summarizing discussions	_____	_____	_____
6. Clarifying issues	_____	_____	_____
7. _____	_____	_____	_____

Figure 3.7 (Continued)

Morale-Building Skills	Doing all right	Need to do it more	Need to do it less
1. Showing interest	_____	_____	_____
2. Working to keep people from being ignored	_____	_____	_____
3. Harmonizing, helping people reach agreement	_____	_____	_____
4. Reducing tension	_____	_____	_____
5. Upholding rights of individuals in the face of group pressure	_____	_____	_____
6. Expressing praise or appreciation	_____	_____	_____
7. _____	_____	_____	_____

Emotional Expressiveness	Doing all right	Need to do it more	Need to do it less
1. Telling others what I feel	_____	_____	_____
2. Hiding my emotions	_____	_____	_____
3. Disagreeing openly	_____	_____	_____
4. Expressing warm feelings	_____	_____	_____
5. Expressing gratitude	_____	_____	_____
6. Being sarcastic	_____	_____	_____
7. _____	_____	_____	_____

Figure 3.7 (Continued)

Ability to Face and Accept Emotional Situations	Doing all right	Need to do it more	Need to do it less
1. Being able to face conflict, anger	_____	_____	_____
2. Being able to face closeness, affection	_____	_____	_____
3. Being able to face disappointment	_____	_____	_____
4. Being able to stand silence	_____	_____	_____
5. Being able to stand tension	_____	_____	_____
6. _____	_____	_____	_____

Social Relationships	Doing all right	Need to do it more	Need to do it less
1. Competing to outdo others	_____	_____	_____
2. Acting dominant toward others	_____	_____	_____
3. Trusting others	_____	_____	_____
4. Being helpful	_____	_____	_____
5. Being protective	_____	_____	_____
6. Calling attention to myself	_____	_____	_____
7. Being able to stand up for myself	_____	_____	_____
8. _____	_____	_____	_____

Figure 3.7 (Continued)

General	Doing all right	Need to do it more	Need to do it less
1. Understanding why I do what I do (insight)	_____	_____	_____
2. Encouraging comments on my own behavior (feedback)	_____	_____	_____
3. Accepting help willingly	_____	_____	_____
4. Making my mind up firmly	_____	_____	_____
5. Criticizing myself	_____	_____	_____
6. Waiting patiently	_____	_____	_____
7. Going off by myself to read or think	_____	_____	_____
8. _____	_____	_____	_____

Source: Reprinted with permission of the National Middle School Association from Elliot Y. Merenbloom, *The Team Process in the Middle School*, 2d ed. (Columbus, Ohio: National Middle School Association, 1986).

One simple and workable solution is to raise these as extended issues. Decide on the spot if they should by necessity or priority supersede the agenda. If the issue is not critical, write it down for the next day's meeting and continue with the day's agenda. In this way, teams guarantee that topics, issues, and concerns, and not an individual's needs, dictate the flow of discussion. This is a small, but powerful issue to be addressed.

Consensus or Majority Vote?

The challenge of staying on task is often coupled with the challenge of resolving disagreements. As effective teams strive for consensus wherever possible, compromise is the watchword. In some instances, an individual teacher's personal philosophy prohibits a consensus from being reached. In such cases, can you rely on the majority vote to resolve the issue? The answer is generally "No." In teams of four, a single decision made with only three out of four votes could haunt the team for an entire school year.

As an example, when attempting to draft a set of team rules and expectations for students, one team could not agree on just how to uphold a single expectation. All the teachers agreed students should be expected to bring paper, texts, and pencils to each and every class. Three out of four believed supplies should not be given to a student who simply forgets. On the contrary, one team member believed this was a judgment call and refused to comply with the supplies denial policy that the rest of the team was advocating. This single issue could drive a wedge into the very heart of the team's harmony.

On such an issue, particularly one that involves student perceptions of staff, a compromise solution is essential. One possible compromise solution is to agree to a trial run for a new policy on the condition that it will be carefully reviewed before being considered for permanent adoption by the team. If consensus cannot readily be reached, more time may be needed for team members to explore their positions on the matter. Ultimately, if no consensus can be reached on some issue, agreeing to disagree may be the best solution. As a result, teachers might enforce different rules in their individual classrooms after informing all their students of these variations. Such an approach is certainly more open than having three people attempting to force a policy down the throat of a resisting fourth team member.

The Reluctant Team Member

After completing her first two months as a team member, one middle school teacher told me, "Not everyone is meant to be a team member. I'd much rather work alone." While most of us are quite reluctant before joining a team for collaborative work, only a small percentage remains as reluctant once teaming is underway. Nonetheless, in every staff there will be some teachers who feel they would rather work alone. For many, this kind of withdrawal from collaborative teaching is avoidable.

Here are a few points to consider:

1. The majority of classroom teachers are extroverts who enjoy thinking, solving problems, and discussing with others (55).
2. Individuals withdraw from group interaction when they perceive themselves to be powerless in that group (33).
3. Historically, schools have not encouraged teacher sharing or collaboration so for many teachers teamwork is a radical departure from their professional past.
4. Practically, many teachers experience tremendous time and work pressures which mitigate against openly discussing new ideas with colleagues.
5. Principals may inadvertently discourage teacher collaboration. In some schools, teachers perceive real sharing to be a departure from the school's norms.
6. Since the majority of teachers are extroverts, many assume that active participation is demonstrated by active dialogue. Yet many of the reluctant team members who are not so inclined need alternative nonverbal avenues for active team involvement.

With these points in mind, involving reluctant team members becomes more manageable. Certainly, an unofficial role assumed by the team's leader (or assigned harmony keeper) might be that of not only soliciting the involvement of the reluctant team member but also arranging appropriate opportunities for involvement. Frequently, these individuals are marvelously skilled in scheduling, organizing, or managing important details that might otherwise be neglected. Appropriately channeled reluctance can be a great asset to an otherwise troubled team.

Exploring a team member's aversion in light of some of the considerations listed above can bring out the reasons for this reluctance. If a member is not blending into the team unit as hoped, it may be because that person views the administration as hostile to teaming, as noted in point 5 above. Knowing that would allow team members to openly discuss the reasons for this view. Open discussion in small groups can be a great healer.

BUILDING TEAM IDENTITY

Once teams have developed a solid organizational foundation for the effective use of planning time, the real substance of teaming comes closer to reality. Almost inevitably teachers begin talking about the students they have in common, sharing concerns, perspectives, and practices. This discussion about students taught in common is a first step toward the creation of a sense of a shared identity. However, the development of team identity deserves deliberate planning. If we expect teaming to make large schools feel small, to reduce school anonymity, and to ensure that students and teachers experience a sense of community, then teams will have to draft plans toward those ends. When interviewing students in one teamed middle school where identity development was not highly valued, we found that most students were not at all aware of the team concept. When asked how she liked her team, one student responded, "What team?"

Planning for identity development is synonymous with planning for the creation of a viable and visible team entity. The possibilities are almost endless, but many teams have found the following suggestions to be a good starting point.

Team Names

Naming is an important and powerful way in which entities are anointed with special character. Small businesses, for example, take great pride in their ingenious names and logos, and successful small businesses can ride on the positive associations their names evoke with future customers. In this respect, teams are no different. Like a family-owned and -operated small business, teams with names are identifiable. This naming process then is a first simple step in building team identity.

The process of selecting a name is rather open-ended. Teachers can go it alone, or they can involve students in some nomination-voting procedure. When teachers decide without involving students, they can select a name that might reflect their team mission or educational philosophy. This name can be carried over from year to year, facilitating a kind of team history. On the other hand, student ownership, combined with the chance of having an unpleasant year, might warrant changing names yearly.

In addition to names, teams generally create identifying logos or symbols with underlying themes. Review these examples of team names and their accompanying themes:

70

Hard Hats	"Learning Under Construction"
All Stars	"Shining with Success"
U.P.S.	"Unlimited Potential and Success"
Private Eyes	"Learning Through Investigation"
Max	"Learning to the Max"

In each case the teams created logos to accompany their themes and names. These logos appeared on team decorations in the team area, on classroom bulletins, on letterhead for team memos and newsletters, and/or emblazoned on tee shirts worn by staff and students.

Team Goals

What does the team hope to accomplish? What goals will characterize the team's mission? Most teams have a guiding set of priorities, whether written or unwritten. Experience with the most successful teams suggests, however, that the clear and careful articulation of goals and priorities is an essential task for teams to perform (30).

Teams vary considerably in the types of goals they choose to endorse. Generally the goals highlight both student and teacher outcomes. First-year teams often begin with very broad goals and tailor them further to their emerging concerns with each passing year of teaming. Keeping a couple of simple guidelines in mind will help ensure that the goals generated are useful. First, keep them few in number. No one can remember eighteen goals at one time, no matter how worthy they seem. By combining, rewriting, editing, and eliminating, a team can produce three or four goal statements, which can truly be useful in guiding the work of the team. Second, a goal does not always have to be concretely measurable, but there should be enough mutual agreement about the meaning of the goal statement that the team members will be able to identify indicators of how well the goal is being accomplished. A composite list of possible team goals appears in Figure 3.8. Not all of these goal statements, copied verbatim from actual statements written by team teachers, guided the work of the same team. But by looking at these statements, one can get some idea of how team goals can relate to a whole range of possible activities. Some goals are rather management-oriented, others relate more to expected

71

Figure 3.8

Team Goals for 19____ — ____

1. Call every parent during the first two weeks of school.

2. End every team meeting ten minutes early.

3. Allow time for grades and progress reports during team time.

4. Limit parent conferences to twenty minutes.

5. Remember to ask for parental input or concerns during first minutes of conference.

6. Always place kids' well-being first on priority list. Use award certificates.

7. Increase communication to all groups (kids, parents, counselors, adminstration, etc.) as a team.

8. Establish and maintain unity and cohesiveness as a team.

9. Get to know each student as an individual.

10. Enjoy the profession we have chosen, and treat each other with mutual trust and respect professionally and personally.

11. Have each child show academic improvement.

12. Have each student show interest about each subject.

13. Help students become self-motivating regarding academic work and citizenship.

14. Know students well enough to make them truly feel this is a small school in a large one.

15. Give each student a positive reinforcement at least once a quarter.

16. Coordinate at least two interdisciplinary units.

17. Communicate and cooperate daily regarding lesson plans and student needs.

18. Emphasize skill development in each subject area.

19. Communicate with Special School District, counselors, and administrators for the best interest of the team's students.

Source: Developed by Parkway East Junior High School, Creve Coeur, Missouri. Reprinted with permission.

student outcomes, and still others focus on high-level teacher interaction. Though all teams do not need to pursue the same goals, every team needs to have its own goals to set it on a journey and to provide the basis for evaluating how far along on that journey the team has been able to travel at some future checkpoint.

It is important to caution teams not to be overly ambitious so that the school year ends with many unfulfilled goals. Such a situation only creates a climate of despair and disillusionment. On the other hand, having team establish a few specific goals that are reasonably achievable will give strength to the entire teaming process.

Team Orientation

The important work of preparing students for the fall school-opening experience is universal. When teaming is in place, however, teachers can develop team-based plans for orienting students. In some schools, students and teachers devote the whole first day to orientation. Others spend several hours during the morning of the first day and begin the afternoon with a shortened version of the academic schedule. In either case students ought to be involved in some form of a team orientation so that they are introduced almost immediately to their team in a rather concrete way. Devoting a half-hour to a team gathering during which the teachers introduce themselves and their goals and all the team's students can literally view themselves as a team can make a lasting impression that is worth the effort. It is also one way to set the precedent for future team activities. Notice that in the sample middle school orientation schedule in Figure 3.9, a team meeting is a significant part of the day.

During the team orientation we recommend including, only briefly, all staff members who serve the team but are not on the team. The principal, assistant principal, guidance counselor(s), physical education staff, special educators, related arts teachers, and media specialists should all stop by the team meeting to introduce themselves. In this way students sense they are enveloped by a caring team community with extended family who are recognizable persons at school.

73

Figure 3.9

Orientation Schedule

I. Building Tour (30 minutes)

  A. Locations

    1. Home Base teacher
    2. Counselor
    3. Attendance
    4. Administration
    5. IMC and computer labs

  B. Support personnel

    1. Attendance
    2. Records
    3. Home-school coordinator

II. Team Meeting (30 minutes)

  A. Location
  B. Time
  C. Introductions

    1. Team members
    2. Counselors
    3. Administrators
    4. Student Council advisor
    5. Librarian and computer

III. Miscellaneous (10 minutes)

  A. Review cafeteria procedure
  B. Review and hand out parent
    information (to be taken
    home)

IV. 8th Grade Visitation (60 minutes)

  A. Pair students

    1. Introductions
    2. Get acquainted

  B. Small group activities

    1. "Know your school"
    2. "People, places, things"

V. Lunch* (30 minutes)

  A. Cafeteria

VI. Breaks* (20 minutes)

  A. Two—10 minutes each

    1. Locations

      a. Grizzlie's Den
      b. Front lawns
      c. Blacktop area

  B. Supervision

    1. Teacher aides
    2. PTA personnel

*Specific times are scheduled for each Home Base.

Source: Developed by North Junior High School, Great Falls, Montana. Reprinted with permission.

Celebrations, Events, and Activities

Once off to a proper start, the team's community life must be massaged and sustained. Team community life depends on regular

74

student and teacher participation in a variety of special activities. Some special activities may be connected with a team topic of study. One team planned a Colonial Day to culminate the social studies unit on the colonial period. Another team planned a team archaeological dig to culminate their study of early human life.

While instructional team activities like these are exceedingly valuable, team activities that are not directly subject-centered but that involve the whole team are particularly effective in cultivating a sense of community. Celebrations of special holidays, such as Halloween, Valentine's Day, and St. Patrick's Day, constitute some of the best and brightest team memories. Moreover, team happenings, such as a special field day, outdoor learning day, craft day, environment day, or peace awareness day, provide opportunities for members to come together in unison.

No doubt team field trips continue to yield remarkable results for teams seeking cohesion. One team leader told me that the team's one-and-a-half-day camping trip was their most solidifying and rewarding team effort. Since taking large numbers of students on a camping trip is not always feasible or desirable, more modest field trips should be considered powerful tools for team cohesion.

As teams have successfully planned and conducted such activities, teachers have reported improved discipline and improved student performance. Positive team experiences do alter the climate of the team and ultimately the climate of the teaching and learning experience. Most importantly, teams that do not take seriously the notion of team community life and that pursue the integration of curriculum as the ultimate end will probably discover many of the technical transformations teaming elicits and not the very people-centered changes that are possible.

So far we have focused on setting a favorable context for successful teaming and on several managerial and group dynamics issues related to promoting positive team interaction. While all this groundwork is important, the real payoff in team organization comes when teachers see how it facilitates their prime function, instruction. In the next two chapters we turn our attention to the ways in which team organization can contribute to more effective teaching.

Chapter 4

DEALING WITH STUDENTS

While team teachers and their students are usually quite delighted with the sense of community that a well-nurtured team can provide (19), teamwork pays the greatest dividends in relation to classroom management and instruction (4). For example, using collaborative planning, teamed teachers can increase the consistency and clarity of the discipline policies and behavior expectations that they apply to students on their teams. Moreover, difficult management situations can be analyzed and resolved in a collaborative fashion, resulting in richer discussions and sounder solutions. Finally, teamed teachers can jointly generate strategies to improve student motivation, student responsibility, and student performance in each of the classrooms represented on the team.

Where teachers have teamed on discipline issues, students seem to sense a unified front. They know that they are part of a caring community in which teachers plan together. At Crabapple Middle School in Atlanta a student reported to an interviewer that teaming meant "that my teachers are ganging up on me." The student's response emphasizes that there was a consistency of expectations, rules, and procedures from classroom to classroom on the team. In teamed settings students do not wander from classroom to classroom where the rules change every hour and where no one seems to know what anyone else is doing. Students do indeed find that the team structure helps them master rules and expectations as well as respond to teacher management strategies that are consistent within the team.

Ideas generated from managing discipline are often matched by collaborative instructional ingenuity. From beginning efforts to identify homework and test schedules to more involved efforts including cross-subject skill development or integrated units, teaming offers almost endless instructional horizons. Teachers can jointly highlight a single skill, diagnose student difficulties, generate plans for instructional improvement, and focus the curriculum more sharply on student needs.

Instructional improvement and effective discipline are unquestionably linked to each other. Through teamwork, teachers gain additional leverage with both domains. In the following pages we will examine several practices in the areas of team management and instruction that teamed teachers have found to be effective.

MOTIVATION, DISCIPLINE, AND STUDENT SUPPORT

Team Rules and Expectations

Team discipline usually begins with a generated and agreed on list of team rules. While these vary from school to school, grade to grade, and team to team, most teams address priorities in the following general areas:

1. Courtesy and respect
2. Preparedness (e.g., supplies, materials)
3. Punctuality
4. Classroom participation
5. Quality of work
6. Care of property.

Some teams involve students in the creation of their final list of rules. While we advocate some degree of student involvement and suggest that Glasser's (33) research endorses such involvement, we would urge the teachers on a team to first establish their baseline rules around which students help build a final list.

Once a reasonable list of baseline rules has been generated, the teachers need to involve students in dialogue in several smaller, class-size groups within the team. At these class-size group discussions the teachers can present the already generated list of baseline rules and lay out the task of refining this list into a set of team rules. Once each of the small team groups agrees on its final list, the teachers should convene a whole-team meeting to determine the final list of rules that will govern the team members.

Knowledge of the team rules and expectations can be promoted in a variety of ways. Many teams send newsletters (Figure 4.1) home to parents, as well as memos to staff members who are not on their team. In addition, as noted in Chapter 2, if teams are appropriately represented on a school-level steering committee, the representative or team leader can further communicate specific

77

Figure 4.1

Sample Team Letter

"HARD HATS"
CAUTION: TEACHERS AT WORK

Dear Parents and Students:

Welcome to "Hard Hats"! We are looking forward to an exciting and constructive school year. With your cooperation and effort, we will build many fun and interesting activities. In order to ensure our success, we have some safety and survival tactics we'd like you to master. Review these this first week so you can help us start off right and pave the road for future fun:

1. Be on time to class.
2. Bring paper, pencil, and notebooks.
3. Walk in our halls.
4. Complete homework.
5. Complete daily work.
6. Seek help when you need it.
7. Give it your best!

We encourage both student and parent conferences and hope to see lots of you during the year. We will be available before and after school hours or during our planning period from 10:10–11:50. Please call your child's Advisor or the Team Leader at 555–3627 to arrange for a conference.

All the best,
The Hard Hats

Mrs. Doda, Leader
Ms. Bomacka
Ms. Reid
Ms. Smith

team discipline information to the school at large. Moreover, the interchange that occurs on the steering committee provides a vehicle to increase schoolwide consistency to some degree among individually operating teams.

Providing the foundation of common team rules and expectations is a necessary first step in promoting positive team discipline. However, sooner or later some students will challenge these rules. Then teachers must decide what to do after infractions have occurred. It is helpful for teamed teachers to have already developed

78

a set of guidelines for dealing with different types of student mis-behaviors. Figure 4.2 represents one team's attempt to develop such a set of guidelines. Vars (77) and Descamps and Lindahl (16) provide further guidance on how teachers with different perspectives can work together on discipline plans. With such a plan, teams can advance the cause of consistency and structure. Over

Figure 4.2
7th Grade Rainbow Team Discipline Plan

When a student receives the fourth detention, she/he is on:

Level 1:

1. Letter sent home to parent expressing team concern.
2. Suspension from all team activities (field trips, movies).
3. Student/team conference.

When a student receives the fifth detention, she/he is on:

Level 2:

1. Parent/student/team conference *or* parent visitation (follows student through the day).
2. Daily teacher conduct card on student—noting behaviors.
3. Weekly conference between student and team member (counselor could be present).
4. One counseling session with guidance counselor.

When a student receives the sixth detention, she/he is on:

Level 3*:

1. Letter to parents requesting parent visitation. If visitation denied, in-team suspension.
2. Administrative conference: student/team counselor/administrator.

When a student receives the seventh detention, she/he is on:

Level 4:

School-level Redline.

*Child can work downward from Level 3 to Level 1.

Source: Developed by the Prince William County Schools, Manassas, Virginia. Reprinted with permission.

time these plans might become so second nature to a team that they require very little time to maintain. However, talking over perspectives on discipline early in the teaming experience can be very rewarding for teachers.

Team Conferencing

Classroom teachers are often faced with the task of conferencing with their students' parents. In addition, many teachers hold conferences directly with their students. With team organization in place, teachers have the opportunity to conduct student and parent conferences as a team. There are clear advantages to this collaborative endeavor. As teachers prepare for a parent conference, they discuss a student from several distinct perspectives. Since student performance varies from subject to subject, and teacher to teacher, such dialogue usually yields a balanced picture of the student. In this sense, team/parent conferencing provides indirect support for students whose performance and behavior are seen in a broader context by the teachers who relate to them daily. Moreover, when four teamed teachers are directly involved in a parent conference, it is less likely that a single teacher will be the recipient of unjust personal blame or criticism. Since the team can portray a balanced view of the child, the parents can be helped to see the positive qualities of their child in the school setting as well as any conditions needing correction or remediation. Parents are more likely to view the teachers as more informed about their child than is often the case at a conference called by a single teacher in response to a problematic situation. In addition, if a child is having difficulties in more than one class, the parents can more easily be helped to face the reality than if they were meeting with each teacher individually.

Not only are team/parent conferences more rewarding for teachers and more supportive for students, but also parents benefit from the collaborative conference because they learn about their child's growth and learning from several teachers' perspectives. Therefore, during a single conference the parents can develop a good overview of how their child is doing in school. In addition, from the parents' point of view, should an individual team teacher have a personality conflict with a student, the impact of this will be diminished in the context of a team conference. Parent conferences tend to be more positive and constructive when the views of several teachers are entered into the discussion.

One of the strengths of productive team/parent conferencing is the preconference team discussion it evokes. Often support staff are involved to offer additional insights into a child's behavior. A conference planning form can be very helpful in focusing this discussion (Figure 4.3). Notice in Figure 4.3 that the conference form includes a place to record a plan. The important thrust here is that the team conference should serve the goal of developing a plan of action designed to remediate the student's difficulties. Without some team system such as this, the team might have trouble with successful follow-up.

In conducting a team/parent conference, teachers should take care not to list all the wrongdoings each one has observed. Ideally, a team spokesperson would report the positive attributes and consolidate the team's concerns so that a parent is not overwhelmed. The practice of starting the conference in this way sets a positive and constructive tone. It is then important to listen to the parents' concerns. Finally, closing the conference with some plan of action for the student to implement is exceedingly important. At this point it is helpful to involve the student in the creation of her or his own plan that will be supported by parents and teachers. With the use of a plan, follow-up is facilitated and desired changes are more likely to occur.

An additional concern with conferencing is the inclusion of relevant staff members from outside the team, such as teachers of elective subjects. While core team members with common planning time can meet to discuss a student in preparation for a conference, nonteam staff who are also involved with the student usually cannot easily attend these meetings because they are assigned to classes during the team meeting time. Here effective teamwork requires adaptive communication measures, such as the form shown in Figure 4.4. This form provides the teacher with a needed vehicle through which perceptions of a student can be shared with a team as they proceed with conference planning.

When teams neglect this critical issue of communication with nonteam staff, these faculty members may become alienated, or even angry. The result can be that the team's work lacks in the depth of perspective that could be provided by teachers in the instructional areas that are not represented by the team's core staff

Figure 4.3
Team Parent Conference Form

Student's Name: _____ Date: _____

Reason for Conference: _____

_____

_____

Parent Concerns: _____

_____

_____

Team Concerns: _____

_____

_____

Student Concerns: _____

_____

_____

Plan: (1) _____

         (2) _____

         (3) _____

Signatures: _____
             Team Representative or Advisor

             _____
             Parent

             _____
             Student

Next Conference or Follow-Up: _____

Figure 4.4

Team Conference Communication

Date: _____

Room: _____

Dear Teacher:

At our team meeting on _____, we discussed _____

_____

We would like to meet with _____ during _____
period on _____ to see if we can come up with a workable plan.
We would like to know which of the topics listed below are of most interest to
you. Please check two or three and add any comments you think are
appropriate. Also, you may add your own topics in the space provided
below.

_____ 1. Punctual to class

_____ 2. Prepared for class

_____ 3. Participates in class

_____ 4. Respectful of others

_____ 5. Responsible

_____ 6. Neat and organized

_____ 7. Obedient of class and school rules

_____ 8. _____

_____ 9. _____

_____10. _____

Please return this letter by _____ so we can consider your
suggestions.
I will come to your class to get the student if that is all right.

Sincerely,

Team Leader

83

of teachers. A student's difficulty with staying seated, for instance, might be further understood by observing his activity level in physical education class. Likewise, a child's success in music might be a clue to his motivation in mathematics. As we discussed in Chapter 2, the team's original structure established during the early development of teaming should include provisions for ongoing communication with teachers who do not teach on the team but nevertheless share some of the same students.

While parent conferencing is the most common form of conferencing, many teams experiment with student conferencing as a means of promoting student involvement in the remediation process. In some cases a team might meet with an individual student to counsel and direct. Depending on the severity of the problem, some means of follow-up is usually instituted. Very often teams rely on a team contract system to help a student monitor his or her own progress. With the contract system the student carries the contract form from class to class and, if successful, requests a teacher's initials on the form. A sample contract form is shown in Figure 4.5. With the help of an assigned team teacher, a discussion of the student's progress can be held at the end of a week.

On the other hand, student/team conferences can also be arranged for celebratory purposes. For example, a team of teachers might choose to call in several of their students in order to praise them for the exemplary contributions they are making to their teams. In some cases teams could also conference with small groups of students, assigning them special tasks or projects that would benefit the team (e.g., decorating bulletin boards, helping new students, mentoring struggling students).

Finally, teams could arrange for student conferences designed to help students with social difficulties or personal hardships that are affecting their performance at school. The process of developing helpful plans can be very supportive for students. It is frequently useful to involve counselors in these conferences. In all cases the collaborative approach creates an embracing system of support and exchange, which facilitates team discipline.

Team Recognition

It is our assumption that a significant number of team discipline problems are rooted in student anonymity. Students who feel un-

Figure 4.5
Team Contact

Name of Student   Advisory Class   Date

Teachers:

Please initial the items indicated only when the student completes the appropriate action for your period.

The student...   1st 2nd 3rd 4th 5th 6th 7th Period

		1st	2nd	3rd	4th	5th	6th	7th
1. is PUNCTUAL to class. (Is on time for class.)	M T W T F							
2. is PREPARED for class. (Has pen, pencil, notebook, text, and other necessary materials.)	M T W T F							
3. PARTICIPATES in class. (Is attentive, involved in classroom activities.)	M T W T F							
4. is RESPECTFUL of others. (Raises hand when needs to talk, is quiet when someone else is speaking, pays attention to the teacher.)	M T W T F							

Figure 4.5 (Continued)

The student...		1st	2nd	3rd	4th	5th	6th	7th	Period
5. is RESPONSIBLE. (Completes assignments on time and turns them in for a grade.)	M T W T F								
6. is NEAT and ORGANIZED. (Writes down assignments, assignments are clean and legible.)	M T W T F								
7. is OBEDIENT of classroom and school rules.	M T W T F								

The student agrees to comply with the above contract for a period of one week. If the student fails to comply with this contract, the parent/guardian will be contacted for a conference.

_____   _____
Team Leader Signature   Student Signature

_____   _____
Date   Date
_____

Source: Developed by the Prince William County Schools, Manassas, Virginia. Reprinted with permission.

known, undervalued, and unrecognized are often the same students who behave in inappropriate ways. Consequently, any effort teams can make to promote student recognition is positive, preventive discipline. Moreover, with the clear relationship between student self-esteem and school achievement (65), team efforts to nurture self-esteem would seem to be critical.

Teams can choose their own appropriate means for recognizing students. The following list of tried practices might prove useful. Many of these ideas have been applied in schools without teaming. In a teamed context, however, they have the advantage of a small, interpersonal environment in which to thrive.

1. Team students of the week, month, semester

2. Birthday celebrations

3. Team honor roll (accompanied by parties, public recognition, buttons, etc.)

4. Special celebratory field trips

5. Awards assemblies each semester to honor many and varied skills, talents, and developments (Examples include Team Poet, Team Sunshine, Team Bookworm, Team Media Whiz, Team Photographer, Team Muscle Man, Team Runner, and so on.)

6. Daily, weekly, and monthly plans to catch students being good, with plans for follow-up recognition (Team games, special notes, team progress reports, and phone calls are all ways in which teams can acknowledge positive student behaviors.)

7. Team area displays of student work and outstanding progress (For example, a team could create a large foot on which they display photos of successful students. The caption could read "Students who are off on the right foot.")

While most of the above examples would certainly be feasible in a nonteamed setting, teacher time is usually the prohibitive factor. However, when teams can conserve time by sharing responsibilities, a range of innovative measures can be employed. It is most important to note here that teams have the rare opportunity to use their collective talents to elevate the attention paid to individual students. Team recognition can systematically promote the positive well-being of the team, but, perhaps more significantly, such recognition can acknowledge more children as special and worthy.

INSTRUCTION

Diagnosis, Evaluation, and Remediation

Effective teaching requires the continuous assessment of student progress with special attention devoted to diagnosing student difficulties, evaluating student achievement, remediating identified difficulties, and placing and regrouping students for instruction. While all these tasks are performed primarily by the individual classroom teacher, the team organization can enhance each process with its collaborative potential.

Interviews with several hundred team teachers confirm that team discussion frequently focuses on students. Teachers who share the same students and the responsibility for instructing those students often talk about those students (19). The resulting dialogue yields increased knowledge of students as both persons and learners and facilitates more responsive instructional management.

As teams discuss students and analyze their performance in various classes, teachers' understandings and insights deepen. The result is that diagnosis is an ongoing dynamic of teaming. This is especially true for children with serious learning difficulties because teams can call on the expertise of special education teachers and counselors who in turn benefit from the rich database a team can generate. In some cases teams might establish a repertoire of successful strategies they can employ with special education students on the team. Under these collaborative conditions, mainstreamed students' needs are satisfactorily met on interdisciplinary teams.

Just as teams can join forces with special education staff, they can enhance their instructional responsiveness by working with other school support staff. When student difficulties emerge in the emotional and social areas, teams can utilize the knowledge and resources of the guidance staff. Regular communication with guidance counselors can facilitate the creation of responsive developmental guidance groups on the team. Moreover, the early discussion of problems with knowledgeable staff might serve to prevent serious crises with troubled students.

Naturally, each team should take advantage of the resources available in the school's media center. Because the media specialist can provide the team with varied resources for instruction and enrichment, it is very helpful to have her or him present at team meetings during which plans for future lessons or units are being discussed. In this way the media specialist becomes an adjunct member of the team, locating and providing appropriate resources to support the unit. Moreover, the media specialist might be a perfect source of support for the unmotivated or reluctant reader, making available reading selections and other helpful experiences.

In addition to holding team diagnostic discussions, teams can enhance evaluation procedures with collaborative efforts. While most teachers value narrative feedback, for example, it is generally difficult for them to find adequate time to write comments for students. Teams can explore ways to share this challenge by dividing the labor fairly. After identifying specific students who clearly need or especially deserve narrative feedback, the team could discuss each student's total progress and assign the narrative writing and consolidation of feedback to an individual team member. Thus, one narrative comment representing all of the team teachers' perspectives would be written for each of the designated students. Team progress reports often replace ones prepared by individual teachers. In this way the team progress report becomes a laborsaving device that still permits teachers to provide narrative feedback to students. A range of similar examples illustrates how team evaluation can work. In our section on team assignments, we will discuss the notion of one assignment with two grades.

Diagnosis and evaluation are ongoing processes in the lives of team teachers. As teachers discuss the daily lives of their students, their knowledge of these students increases in depth and complexity. Out of a concern for equity regarding students, some teams may even develop a calendar of team meetings set aside for serious diagnostic work. In this way teams are guaranteed to address all students equally and fairly. The schedule might include checkpoint meetings at the close of each semester; team members would bring their students' report cards to these meetings for examination and discussion. In the process of holding such meetings, teams can identify needy students and proceed accordingly with appropriate follow-up activities.

Instructional enigmas can be resolved collaboratively. As an example, one elementary school with teacher teams found that there were far too few opportunities for their slower students to complete assignments, review concepts, and acquire assistance. To accommodate these students and their particular needs, the team created an extended academic learning program for students after school. Because it was a team commitment, the supervision responsibility for the three-day-per-week program rotated. Consequently, it was not a great burden for any single teacher. At a later point in time, with the advent of a flexible block schedule, this same school organized what is now called REM, or Reading, Enrichment, and Makeup. This is a flexible instructional time open for team teachers to use as a discretionary time for responsive instructional endeavors.

The notion of a special flexible block of time can be extremely supportive to team teachers. In fact, while it is definitely not a prerequisite to successful teaming, it is an invitation to teachers to further generate responsive instructional plans for students. It is not difficult to imagine a team time being used for team assemblies, guest speakers, special film series, debates, independent study topics, skill-drill groups, literary clubs, and many equally intriguing ideas. These and other examples are appropriately incorporated into the interdisciplinary units that will be discussed in Chapter 5.

Student Grouping

Grouping students in order to facilitate their instruction continues to be a subject of controversy in American education. However, our understanding of the effects of various grouping practices is growing (67, 71). It is very clear from the experiences of schools that have engaged in team organization that students should be grouped onto heterogeneous teams. If each team in the school does not closely reflect the socioeconomic, racial, gender, and ability make-up of the school as a whole, school climate will suffer. If one team comes to be viewed as the "gifted" team, then parents will pressure the principal to assign their children to that team. Teachers will joust among themselves to be assigned to that team. The students on that team will tend to get an inflated view of their self-importance. On the other hand, if a team gets the reputation of being the "dummy" team, parents won't want their children on it, teachers won't want to teach on it, and students' expectations for themselves will suffer. Rigid groupings of students based on any single criterion such as ability should be avoided at all costs when assigning students to teams.

However, once students have been assigned to teams on a heterogeneous basis, they can be grouped and regrouped in various ways to provide effective instruction. The genius of teaming is the flexibility that it provides teachers in making their own decisions regarding the grouping of students. In some cases it is appropriate to use the rich variety of cooperative groups that have been validated by the Johnsons (44) and Slavin (69, 70). Such strategies as Student Teams-Achievement Divisions (STAD), Teams-Games-Tournaments (TGT), Jigsaw II, and Cooperative Learning are designed to take advantage of heterogeneity in the classroom. At other times for certain assignments students can be grouped by interest, social maturity, or motivation as well as by ability.

Some form of ability grouping might be appropriate for certain subjects; when this occurs, teachers can choose from several alternative methods for grouping. On the one hand, Slavin (70) has designed and tested strategies that combine the concept of cooperative groups with within-class ability grouping. For mathematics classes, Team Accelerated Instruction (TAI) has proved effective. In the area of communications skills, Cooperative Integrated Reading and Composition (CIRC) has been found to have a positive influence on student outcomes. If the team teachers desire a more traditional ability-grouped arrangement for sequential subjects, such as mathematics or reading, it is now possible to group students for one or two subjects on a team without inadvertently grouping them in other classes. In nonteamed settings when students are grouped into mathematics classes, they often stay together the whole day, even though mathematics ability makes no sense as a grouping criterion in social studies or English classes. Team organization makes the flexible grouping of students an obtainable objective.

At many schools organized into teams the teachers operate on the assumption that students are initially and randomly assigned to teams and the schedules of students are a team decision. If assigned a group of fifth graders, for instance, the team's teachers will be faced with decisions about the appropriate grouping and scheduling of students for individual classes.

Generally teams must establish a scheduling blueprint, which will dictate their grouping and scheduling parameters. Teams conscious of the inherent problems with tracking and rigid ability grouping (71) might employ a system in which students are ability grouped in no more than two areas, usually language arts/reading or mathematics, and then are heterogeneously grouped for social studies and science.

Ernest Dunning (22), a science teacher on an interdisciplinary team, has developed an easily administered method for grouping students by ability in mathematics, and perhaps language arts, while maintaining heterogeneous groupings in science and social studies. His model, developed for a four-person team with approximately ninety-six students, can be easily adapted for either smaller or larger teams. Dunning's method for grouping and regrouping students is based on the fact that there are only twenty-four possible schedule combinations that a student could follow in a four-hour time block (Figure 4.6). If students on a team are ranked from 1 to 96 based on mathematics ability, they can be grouped into four mathematics classes at different ability levels. However, these students can then be regrouped within the team so that they attend English, social studies, and science in heterogeneous groups. Figure 4.7 displays the student groupings, showing the mathematics classes to be ability grouped and the other classes to be heterogeneous. An extra benefit of using this grouping system is that students do not travel as a unit from teacher to teacher within the team. Consequently, they can interact with a much larger number of students on the team.

In addition to using Dunning's system, teams have the option of addressing the grouping task on a needs basis. As the team plans the curriculum, decisions can be made regarding grouping. If four teachers are serving a fifth grade team, for example, it is quite possible they could share the subject area planning and teaching responsibilities. When they can do so, flexibility in grouping becomes possible. Two teachers, for example, could teach language arts simultaneously. If this were the case, then the fifty to sixty students involved in language arts during any given instructional period could be grouped in any number of ways: by skill deficiencies or strengths, heterogeneously, or perhaps in cooperative learning groups. If a certain number of students needed extensive remediation, one of the team's pair could conduct the skill session, while the other might provide an appropriate enrichment experience for the remaining group of students.

Figure 4.6

Possible Schedule Combinations on a Four-Subject Team

M = Mathematics   E = English   H = History   S = Science

MEHS	HESM	MHES	HMES
EMHS	SEHM	ESMH	SMEH
HEMS	MHSE	HSEM	MSEH
SEMH	ESHM	SHEM	EHMS
MESH	HSME	MSHE	HMSE
EMSH	SHME	EHSM	SMHE

Source: Reprinted with permission of the New England League of Middle Schools from Ernest A. Dunning, "Harmony vs. Discord," *The NELMS Journal* 1, no. 2 (September 1988): 23.

With needs-based grouping, the assumption is that grouping and regrouping are done as needed in response to continuing diagnosis. Some teams might not yet be ready for this challenge. However, experimenting with such internal flexible grouping is an excellent place to start.

Many teaching teams develop a series of pretests that are useful in establishing learning placements at the start of a school year. In this way teachers learn something about the instructional level of the team's students. Often, however, these tests serve to establish permanent ability groups. While we are not advocating such a procedure, initial placements are helpful for teams opting to ability group in language arts and/or mathematics. Research on permanent ability grouping clearly suggests that team teachers frequently evaluate the merit and accuracy of their originally established learning groups.

Figure 4.7

Finished Schedule

	First Period	Second Period	Third Period	Fourth Period
Mathematics	77 78 79 80 81 82 83 84 85 86 87 88 89 90 91 92 93 94 95 96	53 54 55 56 57 58 59 60 61 62 63 64 65 66 67 68 69 70 71 72 73 74 75 76	27 28 29 30 31 32 33 34 35 36 37 38 39 40 41 42 43 44 45 46 47 48 49 50 51 52	1 2 3 4 5 6 7 8 9 10 11 12 13 14 15 16 17 18 19 20 21 22 23 24 25 26
English	2 3 6 7 8 11 12 13 14 16 17 19 23 24 25 26 27 29 30 31 32 41 44 45 49	4 9 15 20 21 33 34 35 37 38 40 43 46 47 48 50 51 52 77 79 80 81 86 88	1 5 10 18 22 53 54 55 56 57 59 61 62 63 64 66 67 69 70 71 72 85 92	28 36 39 42 58 60 65 68 73 74 75 76 78 82 83 84 87 89 90 91 93 94 95 96
History	1 9 10 20 22 33 34 37 38 42 43 48 50 53 54 57 58 61 62 65 66 69 70 73 74	2 3 5 11 12 16 17 18 24 25 28 29 32 36 39 41 49 83 84 89 90 93 94	4 6 7 8 13 14 15 19 21 23 26 60 68 75 76 77 78 81 82 86 87 91 95 96	27 30 31 35 40 44 45 46 47 51 52 55 56 59 63 64 67 71 72 79 80 85 88 92
Science	4 5 15 18 21 28 35 36 39 40 46 47 51 52 55 56 59 60 63 64 67 68 71 72 75 76	1 6 7 8 10 13 14 19 22 23 26 27 30 31 42 44 45 78 82 85 87 91 92 95 96	2 3 9 11 12 16 17 20 24 25 58 65 73 74 79 80 83 84 88 89 90 93 94	29 32 33 34 37 38 41 43 48 49 50 53 54 57 61 62 66 69 70 77 81 86

Each number represents a student ranked by mathematics ability. During first period the low ability (ranks 77–96) class meets. The mathematics classes increase in ability by period until fourth period when the top ability group meets (ranks 1–26). The English, science, and history classes contain mixed ability groups. Students attend classes with a wide variety of students on the team. For example, student #1 attends classes with sixty-eight of the ninety-six students represented here.

Source: Reprinted with permission of the New England League of Middle Schools from Ernest A. Dunning, "Harmony vs. Discord," *The NELMS Journal* 1, no. 2 (September 1988): 26.

Assignments

It should be clear at this point that team teachers can coordinate relevant instructional tasks in ways that support the instructional program but do not require curriculum integration. In addition to diagnostic teamwork and consequent remediation, teams discover that they can provide a more coherent and manageable instructional program when they coordinate assignments. Calendars noting subject area tests, homework projects, and other special assignments can be created and shared to avoid conflicts or student overload. When they have a team schedule of major assignments, all teachers can provide the appropriate encouragement, supporting student progress across the board.

Teaming teachers can also collaborate on a single assignment. Why, for example, should both the language arts and the social studies teachers assign and grade separate written reports? A single report could be prepared, representing both the social studies content and the language arts skill requirements. With such a single assignment, students begin to see language arts as applied skills that are useful in many areas of knowledge. Furthermore, the preparation of a single report might increase the quality of student work.

When major tests must be given on the team, teachers might explore additional collaborative opportunities. Provided the team has a flexible block schedule, the team's teachers could facilitate test taking by devoting the first period to a teamwide science test, for instance, followed by a second/third period team activity. During the large group team event the science teacher would be free to grade papers. In this way students could receive immediate feedback and teacher time would be saved.

Instructional Overlap

Moving from instructional coordination to plans for student learning, team teachers have the option to collectively target key instructional goals. For example, teams might begin to identify cross-subject skills and habits they would like to foster in the students they have in common. Certainly, addressing spelling, writing, skimming, proofreading, listening, handwriting, reflective thinking, outlining, and any similar generic learning skills would prove beneficial to learners in all areas of study. When teachers

95

plan instruction collaboratively on teams, they can reinforce skills in several subject areas. Good paragraph construction originally taught in English class can be reinforced through coordinated assignments in science and social studies. The effect of this instructional collaboration is a sharper focus on particular skills that tends to emphasize their importance in the minds of students. Improved achievement soon follows.

Beyond the shared assignment idea and the skill focusing, teams can further overlap with regard to content. While fully integrated content is examined in Chapter 5, here it is appropriate to suggest modest attempts to overlap from one subject area to the next. The study of ancient Greece in social studies could be complemented by the study of Greek mythology in language arts. Similarly, the study of the weather in science might be appropriately complemented by the study of poetry and prose in language arts or by the study of human adaptation in social studies. Examples are numerous. Certainly, some shifting of curriculum calendars might be necessary. This will often be the deciding factor for interested teachers. When weighing the decision regarding possible overlap, teachers ought to balance the concern for content sequence in social studies, for example, with the benefit of skill reinforcement for students. There is simply no one best way to sequence school subjects. Team teachers have quite a bit of discretion regarding the scheduling of instructional units.

Where teams ambitiously pursue opportunities for overlap and take advantage of these lucky links, a rich array of complementary activities is usually available to students. Team academic assemblies, debates, trips, special events, and coordinated content lessons and assignments all represent efforts in this domain. More specifically, consider the following illustrative examples of team efforts:

1. *Scientific Method Madness*: An entire team would focus on the application of the scientific method for full week. Each team teacher would prepare several individual lessons in which he or she applies the scientific method to his or her particular subject area.

2. *Writer's Cramp Week*: Shifting to an emphasis on English-/language arts, a team might devote its collective energies to writing. In all subject areas teachers would prepare

96

lessons and activities designed to enhance writing skills, thus reinforcing what students would be learning in language arts. In this example it is easy to imagine ways in which writing as a form of communication might be employed in all areas.

3. *Environmental Awareness*: Because of our ongoing concern for the environment and the resulting attention paid to this critical area in the social sciences, many teams have created lessons that address this broad issue. In language arts, students might prepare a debate, write letters to public officials, interview scientists, and participate in other similar activities. Mathematics might involve students in graphing environmental changes over time, in different regions, and so on. Certainly science lessons would not be difficult to project, including lessons on erosion, pollution, ozone depletion, and other related topics. Finally, social studies lessons could highlight any number of issues, including pesticides, diseases, food toxins, and many social issues. The week or so could culminate with a march for environmental protection, a team aluminum can drive, or some other special closing activity.

Examples of such overlapping features are endless. The creative possibilities inherent in a team of professionals should open instructional doors that might otherwise remain closed. In Chapter 5 we will look at curriculum integration in more detail.

Chapter 5

TEACHING WITH
INTERDISCIPLINARY UNITS

Education is the acquisition of the art of the utilization of knowledge.
(79, p. 16)

In the previous chapter we began to show how teaching on an interdisciplinary team can help teachers deal with the eternal question "How can we motivate these students?" Through joint planning and flexible scheduling, teachers can do a more effective job of organizing instruction that addresses students' needs. There is one further step that can provide the most comprehensive way yet devised to make learning relevant to students, adjust it to varying interest and ability levels, and provide an enjoyable experience for both teachers and students. This "miracle cure" for our teaching blahs is the Interdisciplinary Thematic Unit (ITU).

Interdisciplinary thematic units constitute the most comprehensive instructional strategy in the repertoire of many teams. For experienced team teachers they represent the most satisfying way in which to achieve curricular integration. Well-planned ITUs are organized around important themes or problem-solving situations that call on students to integrate the knowledge and skills they are being asked to master in the various subjects taught on the team. Interdisciplinary thematic units are generally designed to include a balance of teacher-directed instruction, small group work, and individual activities. Such units lend themselves well to meeting the needs of students with varying interests and ability levels. In addition, the joint planning that such units require allows the teachers on a team to divide the labor in order to take advantage of their different strengths.

Though ITUs are the most sophisticated means for integrating curricula, they are not the only way to take advantage of team collaboration to make instruction more effective and enjoyable for learners (76). Interdisciplinary thematic units represent the fourth level on a four-level continuum of curricular integration practiced on teams. These levels are defined in terms of the amount of joint instructional planning required by the team teachers in order to carry out the integrative activities.

Level one can be labeled *preintegration*. It refers to the flexible scheduling that is possible on a team to provide for variation in lesson planning. For example, teachers organized on teams can alter their teaching schedules to provide for field trips, films/videos, outside speakers, teamwide assemblies, or laboratory experiences. While no true integration of curriculum may be taking place, instruction is improved by fitting activities to their more natural time requirements rather than trying to fit every lesson into a 45- or 50-minute period. This flexible scheduling also encourages teachers to use a greater variety of instructional strategies that seem appropriate for students on the team.

Level two might be called *coordinated or overlap teaching*. Coordinated teaching refers to the practice of teaching related topics, lessons, or units at the same time. For example, if the English teacher is teaching myths at the same time the social studies teacher is teaching about ancient Greece, or if the science teacher is teaching a unit on inventions at the same time the social studies teacher is teaching about the Industrial Revolution, we have overlap teaching. Coordinated teaching requires a minimum amount of collaborative planning in order to achieve some curricular integration. About the only requirements for accomplishing this type of curricular coordination are (1) familiarity with the topics or units being taught by the other members of one's team and (2) willingness to move a related unit in one's own subject area to coincide with that being taught by a teammate.

The third level on the integration continuum can be labeled *cooperative teaching*. This level requires two or more teachers to make changes in how they teach some topic in order to mutually reinforce their various subjects. A good example of cooperative teaching that is practiced on many teams is the "skill of the week." An English teacher might be emphasizing paragraph development through the use of topic sentences and supporting detail. Sometime during that week the teachers of all the other subjects taught on the team would assign an activity that requires students to apply the skills being learned in English. Other examples of cooperative teaching include an English teacher creating a literature unit to reinforce a social studies unit on the 1930s and a science teacher and a social studies teacher rearranging their instruction to coordinate the study of astronomy and space with the study of space exploration in the 1960s. Cooperative teaching is distinguished from coordinated teaching by the fact that it requires more joint planning and more flexibility regarding instructional decision making. However, the positive outcomes can be greater because there is a more deliberate effort on the part of the teachers to plan for the reinforcement of their various subjects throughout the team.

The *interdisciplinary thematic unit* takes the level of joint planning and integration of subject matter a step further. To develop an ITU, two or more teachers on a team plan a unit of instruction that fully integrates their several subjects around a unifying theme or problem to be solved. While a typical unit might take about two weeks to teach, the length of time is not a crucial element in the design of a unit. Some are designed to be taught for shorter periods and others for longer periods—even up to a full year. A seventh grade team in Paola, a small town in eastern Kansas, built its curriculum for an entire school year around a community service project: raising money to restore the four-faced courthouse clock at the county seat (Figure 5.1). Few ITUs are as involved as the one taught in Paola. However, their execution can be made more successful if teachers understand a few simple characteristics of ITUs.

CHARACTERISTICS OF INTERDISCIPLINARY THEMATIC UNITS

If teachers take five factors into account, they can increase the probability that the units they design will be more successful in meeting diverse learner needs, promoting increased learning, and being more enjoyable learning experiences for both students and teachers. A good ITU grows out of the basic curriculum; it is not just a fun diversion for a couple of weeks.

A Wide Variety of Instructional Objectives

An ITU must be grounded in the curricular objectives that are expected to be taught in the various subject areas included on the team. A good thematic unit will be based on a wide variety of in-

Figure 5.1

Clock Restoration Unit

When the seventh grade team at Paola Middle School recently completed an interdisciplinary thematic unit, they did it in grand style with Governor John Carlin and Supreme Court Justice Robert Miller on hand. Over a year ago the seventh grade team at Paola Middle School, headed by Verla Thomas and consisting of Kim Hawkins, Norlene Rhinehart, Connie Ballew, and Penny Sipe, decided to organize a thematic unit centered around a community project. When the Miami County Courthouse was renovated several years ago, the four-faced tower clock was cut from the project because of cost.

Last year the seventh grade team made raising the $13,000 to restore the clock the focal activity of a unit on "Community Pride." The students studied the history of Miami County and its courthouse, clocks in general, and cost factors in the nineteenth century and now, as well as working on oral and written communications skills. The seventh graders carried out a variety of fund-raising activities in the pursuit of their goal: quilt raffle, variety show, country-western concert, and business solicitations.

Last September 28 the year's effort paid off for the seventh grade team when the community dedicated the new clock in ceremonies attended by state officials. The middle school choir and bands were also involved as they provided music for the event. The local newspaper published a special tabloid section devoted to the restoration project.

The Paola seventh grade team and the school's principal Olin McCool have provided a concrete example to illustrate that learning can be relevant and fun when the hard work is related to meaningful goals. The boundless energy of early adolescents can indeed be channelled into productive learning by caring, competent teachers working together on teams.

Source: KAMLE Tracks: Newsletter of the Kansas Association for Middle Level Education (Fall 1980). Reprinted with permission.

structional objectives. Not only should the unit contain objectives related to the basic skills, knowledge, and concepts that are to be taught in the various subject areas, but also a complete unit can easily address some of those other objectives that we say are important for the education of young people: objectives related to group process skills, critical thinking skills, problem-solving skills, positive attitude development, self-knowledge, and positive self-esteem. A unit that is too narrowly focused on just a few basic skills objectives will miss the real opportunity to take students beyond the mastery of the basics toward the application of those skills in some type of real-life activity.

Romance, Precision, and Generalization

An effective ITU will be built around the concept that learning is cyclical and rhythmic. A well-planned unit embodies the notion that the learning cycle consists of romance, precision, and generalization. These ideas were first articulated in the 1910s and 1920s by British educator, mathematician, and philosopher Alfred North Whitehead in his essays collected in *The Aims of Education* (79). Whitehead argued that learning begins when learners become aware that there is something out there to learn that has real potential to improve their understanding and skill. Whitehead attempted to capture the essence of the romance stage of the learning cycle with this reference to Robinson Crusoe:

> Crusoe was a mere man, and the sand was mere sand, the footprint was a mere footprint, and the island a mere island, and Europe was the busy world of men. But the sudden perception of the half-disclosed and half-hidden possibilities relating Crusoe and the sand and the footprint and the lonely island secluded from Europe constitutes romance. (79, p. 29)

Romance is the stage of learning during which the learner becomes excited about the possibilities in learning something new. We often refer to this idea when we talk about the "motivation" activities at the beginning of a lesson or unit of instruction.

If the romance stage is successful, students are then ready to move to the precision stage, which requires them to master new material, learn the grammar, grasp new procedures, memorize the facts, comprehend the relationships among concepts, and generally learn the basics. However, if instruction ends here, as it often does in school-based instruction, the learning cycle is cut short, preventing students from seeing the relevance of the material they have mastered to any meaningful application in their lives. The complete learning cycle requires a stage of generalization during which students apply what they have learned to new situations. Students in some way use what they have learned to create something new or demonstrate their knowledge by producing some product using the principles and skills they have learned. Whitehead criticized

102

schools sixty years ago for placing too much emphasis on the precision stage of learning. We teachers go forth to require mastery before students have accepted the importance of what we are asking them to learn. Then we abort the learning cycle by terminating learning in a multiple-choice, matching, or fill-in-the-blank test. There is seldom any opportunity for students to use what they have learned in any meaningful way. However, teachers can intentionally plan for romance, precision, *and* generalization when they create an ITU.

Teachers can plan for generalization if they use the trick of planning the unit backwards by starting with the end. During their planning discussions the teachers need to decide what it is that they would like students to be able to do or produce at the end of the unit of instruction. By planning the culminating activities first, the teachers are assured that the unit will lead to generalization rather than ending prematurely during the precision stage. Kierstead (51, 52), an experienced teacher, does an excellent job of describing the process of planning backwards from what she calls "long-term goals" and "real-life products." Though a test can be used to help evaluate some of the outcomes of a unit, what makes teaching with units such a powerful idea is that students, working individually or in small groups, are required to create some product or plan some performance that compels them to integrate the skills and knowledge they are learning in each of the subject areas taught on the team. Their learning takes on an immediacy that is hard to duplicate with traditional teaching strategies. Nothing is more motivating for most students than to appear competent in front of their peers. If a unit of instruction culminates in a product to be displayed publicly or in a performance to be viewed by peers and perhaps others (e.g., parents, other students, or community members), students will have a built-in motivation that many will not have if the most significant outcome of a unit of instruction is just another test. Figure 5.2 contains some suggested real-life activities that could be used to culminate an ITU.

A Really Important Theme

Another crucial factor in designing an ITU is to select a really important theme to provide a focus for the unit. A good theme should have at least these two characteristics: (1) it should be an

Figure 5.2

Ideas for Culminating Activities:
Alternatives to the Test for Being Accountable

1. Videotape productions (with or without a tape)
   a. "60 Minutes" TV magazine format
   b. Newscast
   c. Spoof of some popular TV show format

2. Multimedia projects (combining an oral presentation with music; skits; filmstrips; or student-produced slides, tapes, or pictures)

3. Models
   a. Life-size
   b. Miniature

4. Displays
   a. Museum displays (combining artifacts and written explanations)
   b. Collages
   c. Photos
   d. Drawings

5. Personalized projects
   a. Autobiographies
   b. Family trees

6. Action plans
   a. Letter writing
   b. Visitations
   c. Sending recommendations for change to some appropriate agency*
   d. Carrying out some community service project

7. Add your own ideas
   a.
   b.
   c.
   d.

---

*As a culminating activity to a unit on government, a group of seventh graders in Arizona began a campaign that eventually led to the amending of the Arizona state constitution. For more details, see Clark's "Changing the Arizona Constitution" (14).

umbrella that facilitates the integration of all subjects proposed for inclusion in the unit, and (2) it should be significant and intrinsically interesting. If the theme that we choose to give our unit life violates one of these principles, it will cause problems for us during the teaching of the unit.

Taking a theme from our textbooks can get us in trouble. For example, one team attempted to organize a unit around the theme of "Greece." While the social studies curriculum might require students to study the country of Greece, "Greece" does not lend itself to being a theme for an ITU. In the first place, it may be a rather poor umbrella for some subjects. What legitimate mathematics objectives could fit under this topic? Second, how many students in modern America would find "Greece" such a hot topic that they couldn't resist plunging into studying about it?

More promising themes are those that are both broad enough to comfortably include objectives from all subject areas and significant enough for students to relate to. What White and Bennett (78) call the "grand realities" lend themselves to being integrative themes for students: power, change, faith, oppression, work, passion, authority, beauty, violence, love, and prestige. Other themes that relate to students' lives can work well: exploration, independence, human rights, interdependence, heroes, energy, the future, and ecology. Though the unit must be grounded in the real curricular objectives of the subjects to be included in the unit, the theme itself must raise students' sights above the mundane so that they are helped to see that the "nitty-gritty" they are being asked to learn does relate to something wondrous.

Balanced Activities

A good thematic unit also provides for a balance between teacher-structured and student-structured activities. The teachers will control the long-term goals for the unit; they will negotiate with students on short-term goals, allowing some student choice among alternatives; and they will permit students to regularly control the minute-by-minute decisions regarding pace, sequence, and content when the teacher is not engaged in direct instruction. Kierstead (51, 52) described more fully how teachers can integrate teacher-led direct instruction with student-controlled activities, including the use of cooperative groups (44, 69, 70).

The Soars (72) have explained why a teacher would want to share control of the learning tasks in a classroom. The relationship between teacher control of the learning tasks and student learning is not a linear one. Only up to a certain point do teacher planning and control of student learning behavior lead to more student learning. Beyond that point, continued teacher structuring inhibits student learning. The Soars (72) have called this phenomenon the "Inverted U" relationship (Figure 5.3). Teachers conscious of the push to increase student achievement need to be aware that they can, indeed, overstructure student learning activities if they do not allow students the opportunity to exercise judgment and make decisions that affect the outcome of the learning activities.

Figure 5.3

Teacher Control vs. Student Growth:
The "Inverted U" Relationship

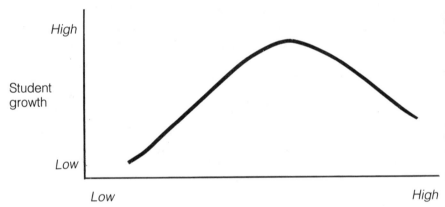

Note: By placing one's hand over the right half of the graph, the reader can see where the idea comes from that increased teacher control of learning tasks is associated with increased student learning. However, by removing one's hand again, one can see that this notion is true only up to a point. Beyond that point, *increased* teacher control of learning tasks has been found to be associated with *decreased* student learning.

Source: Reprinted with permission of the American Association of Colleges for Teacher Education from Robert Soar and Ruth Soar, "An Attempt To Identify Measures of Teacher Effectiveness from Four Studies," *Journal of Teacher Education* 27, no. 3 (Fall 1976): 261–67.

A *Wide Variety of Student Learning Activities*

A final characteristic of an effective ITU is that it employs a wide variety of student learning activities. This particular characteristic is readily facilitated by team planning. Since two to five teachers may be involved in the planning of an ITU, not only can they brainstorm a wide variety of learning activities, but also they can organize the unit to cater to their own strengths and preferences. They can plan the unit so that students will experience many different types of activities, but each teacher might have to lead only a portion of these. The ITU provides an excellent vehicle for satisfying the needs of diverse learners. The teachers who plan together can assure that students will experience a variety of learning strategies during the team instructional time, even if they don't experience each alternative in any one class. Because the possibilities are limitless, it is not difficult for several teachers planning together to provide opportunities for students to experience individual work, cooperative groups, simulations, instructional games, computer-assisted instruction, library research, student presentations, whole-class discussions, media presentations, learning centers, and teacher-led mini-lectures, all within a two-week period. Such variety would do much to break the cycle of sameness that Goodlad (34) described as sapping the enjoyment from learning for so many students.

Making provisions for including these five characteristics in the design of an ITU can make teaching such a unit a truly exciting experience. It will not only nurture the teacher's professional growth but also energize students to achieve in ways that teachers have only dreamed about in the past. In a previously published work (17), one of the authors described eleven positive outcomes that she discovered as the result of teaching an ITU (see Figure 5.4).

TIMING—ANOTHER KEY TO SUCCESS

Another issue that does not fit neatly under the title of characteristics, or steps in planning, but which is important, is when to fit an ITU into the annual cycle of the academic year. Some units are designed to be taught at the beginning of the year. These units can combine an emphasis on the romance of learning on the team with an introduction to study skills. Such a unit is also a good ve-

107

Figure 5.4
What We Discovered

In spite of the frustrations along the way, the unit's success was overwhelming. We happily discovered:

1. Students who were turned off to Language Arts and Reading were newly motivated and worked enthusiastically.

2. Students engaged in self-initiated projects related to but not required by the unit's activities (i.e., a small group designed and built an airport for the future).

3. Students acknowledged the application of skills to practical situations (i.e., the need to read directions carefully before filling out a job application).

4. As a result of increased student interest, all but a few students received higher grades. They were pleased with their success.

5. Teaching became more exciting as we shared our successes and failures with each other. The experience encouraged each of us to examine our own teaching strengths and weaknesses.

6. The nature of the unit allowed for student freedom but fostered student self-discipline.

7. With two of us at work, student needs were met more effectively. One could work with a small group while the other facilitated those working individually.

8. The unit involved the Math and Science teachers on our team. They enriched the unit as visiting instructors and taught related large group lessons.

9. Those skills selected to be taught were successfully taught as suggested by a final post-test evaluation.

10. Students learned to work together democratically and were pleased to see their teachers cooperating for their welfare.

11. Students were able to work continuously on one integrated learning experience and felt they accomplished more as a result.

Source: Reprinted with permission of the National Middle School Association from Nancy Doda, *Teacher to Teacher* (Columbus, Ohio: National Middle School Association, 1981), 36–37.

hicle for introducing students new to teaming to the idea that they will be studying with a group of teachers who will be planning together for their learning. Other units are planned for the end of the year. Here the emphasis can be on pulling together, reviewing, and extending skills and knowledge learned throughout the school year. Since such a unit is organized around high-interest, hands-on activities and problem-solving situations, it would be ideal for keeping students motivated at the end of the year when their fancies would otherwise turn to less academic concerns.

Other units can be planned to fit in with seasonal events. Teachers might take advantage of good weather in the spring or fall for some outdoor-related themes. Various holidays might lend themselves to units built around such themes as caring, sharing, friendship, remembering, past human struggles, exploring, human rights, and human relationships to nature. Recurring events, such as elections or the Olympic Games, can provide motivating theme possibilities. One-time or serendipitous events of a local, national, or international nature can also provide excellent opportunities for the team that is in tune. The courthouse clock restoration referred to earlier (Figure 5.1) is a good example of building a unit around a local opportunity. Such recent events as the traveling King Tut exhibit, the airing of "Roots," the Mount St. Helens eruption, and the Armenian earthquake could form the basis of an ITU that would appeal to the curiosities of young learners.

STEPS IN THE PLANNING PROCESS

There is no one perfect way to plan an ITU. Several methods for the team planning of units have been discussed previously by other authors (17, 31, 42). We can offer some additional suggestions based on the experience of classroom teachers who have successfully carried out ITUs on their teams. A well-designed ITU combines team planning with individual planning. Since the chief curricular purpose of teaching an interdisciplinary unit is the integration of subject matter, some decisions must obviously be made jointly by the entire team. However, since each team member is responsible for teaching the curriculum in one or more subject areas, each teacher must make some planning decisions based on specific expertise. This section will clarify those decisions that the team must make in order for the individual members to complete the planning for the unit in each of their subject areas. An outline of the planning steps is presented in Figure 5.5.

The team as a whole must make three major decisions. These decisions cannot easily be made in any sequential order. Since all three affect each other, they need to be considered at the same time by the whole team. The first of these joint decisions involves the activity or activities that will culminate the unit. What kinds of real-life products or performances will students carry out to show what they have learned in the unit? Will these final products result from cooperative group activities or from individual efforts? However, before closure can be reached on the appropriate culminating activities, teachers must settle on a theme. If the theme is related to some kind of community service, then the culminating activities may even take place outside of school time. Who will the audience be for the theme's culminating activity—the team itself, the town council, younger students in the school, parents, or local radio listeners or television viewers?

Figure 5.5

Steps in Planning an Interdisciplinary Thematic Unit

The team as a whole has joint responsibility for these first three decisions. They are to be discussed *at the same time* during the romance stage of unit planning rather than being considered sequentially.

1. Decide on the culminating activity.
2. Decide on the theme.
3. Decide on two or three unifying instructional objectives.

During the following steps the decision-making responsibility shifts to the individual teachers on the team. However, they continue to talk to each other to gain input for their particular decisions.

4. Select the subject area objectives that will be taught during the unit.
5. Select and sequence a variety of student learning activities.
6. Plan for student accountability.

The final steps require continued interaction among individual teachers to complete a successful unit.

7. Prepare for instruction.
8. Begin teaching the unit, revising as appropriate.
9. Evaluate the unit.
10. Add the unit to your team teaching repertoire to use again.

In addition to deciding on the culminating activities and the theme, the team teachers should decide jointly on two or three integrating objectives. These instructional objectives should emphasize the relationships among subjects, group process skills, higher-order thinking, self-esteem building, and other legitimate instructional objectives that go beyond the limits of any one subject area to provide an integrated focus for the unit.

Considering these three factors as a team will allow the teachers to do some romancing with each other. This is an exciting time in the planning of a unit. There is so much potential; there are so many possibilities. Allowing flights of fantasy over various themes and possible culminating activities gets the team's creative juices flowing. It is all right not to rush to closure at this point in the planning process. The more ideas that get put on the table for consideration, the greater the likelihood that the decisions eventually made will be good ones.

After several days of discussion, the team members will have to decide on the culminating activity, the theme, and the integrating objectives. Once this is done, the unit has a direction and a focus to it. However, much individual planning still needs to take place. Remembering that the unit must carry out some curricular objectives that are expected to be taught in the various subject areas, each teacher must now analyze the culminating activity (remember to plan backwards) to determine what subject-specific objectives will be taught as part of the unit. Each teacher must decide which skills, concepts, and processes will be contributed to the unit by English or science or mathematics or social studies. Along with considering objectives, each teacher must decide what learning activities students will need to experience to prepare them for the culminating activity. Individual teachers have final responsibility for deciding on the activities and objectives within their own subject areas. However, as they are considering their options, they should share their thoughts with the rest of the team. In that way further coordination can take place, and perhaps new insights will occur.

Another issue that teachers must address, both individually and jointly, is how students are to be held accountable for their work. Will aspects of the culminating activity be graded jointly by two or more teachers? Will there be some products or performances for which group grades as well as individual grades will be given?

What types of formative evaluations will be conducted during the unit within the separate subject areas? Will students be involved in the evaluation of group work or in the evaluation of other students' final products? There are no right answers here. However, evaluation and grading take on a new dimension when they are part of an ITU.

The final steps in the planning process for ITUs are very similar to the steps that any teacher would follow when carrying out a unit of study. The major difference is that teachers are working together, which permits brainstorming, emotional support, division of labor, and a sense of camaraderie that is often lacking when teachers plan instruction alone. For the record the final four steps are these: (1) prepare for instruction; (2) begin the unit, revising as needed; (3) evaluate the unit; and (4) revise the unit, and add it to your team's repertoire so that you can use it again next year. During the planning and preparation stages, team teachers must not forget to coordinate their work with the specialists with whom they work. Library/ media specialists can be very helpful in preparing to teach an ITU and need to be involved early in the process. Special education teachers with whom the team shares students also need to be involved early so that they can help plan the modifications that will make the unit appropriate for the special students on the team. What about the counselor, the social worker, and the nurse? Will they be involved? Once the unit is underway, teachers can use the regular team meeting to exchange information on how things are going so that suitable ''on-line'' revisions can be made.

Planning a successful ITU is not a casual undertaking. This is why it is generally not recommended as a top priority for a new team. It takes one to three years of working together, getting to know each other's personalities, and getting to know something about each other's subjects before an ITU can be planned without undue stress and frustration. In the meantime team teachers can move toward interdisciplinary units by trying flexible scheduling, coordinated or overlap teaching, and cooperative teaching. After a year or two of working together, team teachers will be better prepared to tackle the professional challenge of integrating subject matter and presenting it to students in an intrinsically interesting way.

Figure 5.6

Bibliography of
Interdisciplinary Thematic Units

This bibliography provides representative descriptions of interdisciplinary thematic units. In most cases the descriptions were written by the teachers who were involved in creating the units described. Also discussed are other issues relating to unit planning, including some alternatives to those presented in this chapter.

James A. Beane, Conrad F. Toepfer, Jr., and Samuel J. Alessi, Jr., "An Illustrative Interdisciplinary Resource Unit: Living in the Future," in *Curriculum Planning and Development* (Boston: Allyn and Bacon, 1986), 401–17.

This resource unit provides a complete model for developing an ITU. It contains the following sections: rationale statement, objectives, student activities related to the objectives, resources, measuring devices (including self-evaluation), and a description of a cooperative learning method.

Louise C. Bell, "Learning Centers in the Classroom," *Middle School Journal* 14, no. 2 (February 1983): 17–19.

Though this article does not describe a full unit, it provides ideas that can be adapted in order to include learning centers among the student activities in an ITU.

Melvyn A. Brodsky, "The Roaring Twenties: An Interdisciplinary Unit— Or How To Make Use of That Old Raccoon Coat in the Attic," *Middle School Journal* 18, no. 4 (August 1987): 7–9.

The genesis of this unit was the Stock Market Game. It grew to involve not only the basic interdisciplinary team but also most of the related arts teachers as well. Described is an excellent example of romance to begin the unit. Also included are the major student activities and the evaluation scheme.

Francine Buckingham, Lucille Jordan, and Shirley S. Scholl, "There Is No Finish Line: The Story of a Successful Interdisciplinary Unit Carried Out by 'Amateurs,'" *Middle School Journal* 18, no. 2 (February 1987): 18–19.

From the romance of the opening ceremonies to the generalization of the closing ceremonies, the Olympics provided the theme for a broad-based unit involving English, science/health, social studies, and mathematics. This unit also involved several community agencies.

113

Figure 5.6 (Continued)

Timothy Daniels, Joseph O'Brien, and Robert Pittman, "Interdisciplinary Units—Keystones of Learning," *Middle School Journal* 13, no. 3 (May 1982): 14–16.

This article describes the rationale, objectives, and "nuts and bolts" of three units, each of which gets students out of their school building and into their larger environment: tracing the life of a local river, visiting an environmental center, and studying the urban area around them. The relationship of team organization to ITUs is also discussed.

Anne Wescott Dodd, "Try a Total School Effort To Improve Student Writing," *Middle School Journal* 16, no. 3 (May 1985): 8–10.

Though not a description of a single unit, this article provides many ideas that are well suited for use by an interdisciplinary team to reinforce writing skills.

Thomas O. Erb, "Structure for Openness: An Eighth Grade Unit on Exploration," *Opening Education for Children and Youth* 6, no. 2 (Winter 1979): 24–27.

This article provides a fairly detailed description of the thought processes that the teachers went through in designing the unit as well as a description of how students interacted during the teaching of the unit. Emphasis is placed on balancing teacher structure with student decision making.

Mary E. Hass, "Learning from an Old Mail-Order Catalogue: A Resource Unit on Change in America," *Middle School Journal* 19, no. 2 (February 1988): 22–24.

A reprint of the old 1908 Sears and Roebuck catalogue inspired this unit, which illustrates many elements of successful units: broad objectives, varied student activities (including individual and group work), and an evaluation that provided for generalization.

Alan H. Humphreys, Thomas R. Post, and Arthur K. Ellis, *Interdisciplinary Methods: A Thematic Approach* (Santa Monica, Calif.: Goodyear Publishing Co., 1981).

Fourteen interdisciplinary units are outlined in detail in this book. Additional ideas for interdisciplinary teaching using a thematic approach are discussed.

Joanne Kerekes, "The Interdisciplinary Unit. . .It's Here To Stay!" *Middle School Journal* 18, no. 4 (August 1987): 12–14.

114

Figure 5.6 (Continued)

This article describes how ITUs fit into the life of an interdisciplinary team. Special emphasis is placed on one particular unit built around the theme of the "Fabulous Fifties."

Phyllis S. Levy, "Webbing: A Format for Planning Integrated Curricula," *Middle School Journal* 11, no. 3 (August 1980): 26–27.

Three different approaches to using webbing are discussed. Webbing is a very useful technique that can be used to structure an ITU so that the various subjects fit together.

M. Jill Streit and Carol D. Schnurstein, "The Journal of the Teamship Holmes: Survival in an Interdisciplinary Habitat," *Middle School Journal* 15, no. 2 (February 1984): 18–21.

A whole building of twenty-eight teachers functioned as a team to involve 400 students in an "Endangered Species" unit that led them to the wilderness area of a nearby state park and to the local zoo. Physical education, foreign languages, home economics, art, and music were integrated with language arts, social studies, science, and mathematics in this unit. The logistics of planning and conducting this unit are discussed along with its content.

Robert B. Stromberg and Joan M. Smith, "The Simulation Technique—Applied in an Ancient Egypt I.D.U.," *Middle School Journal* 18, no. 4 (August 1987): 9–11.

Simulations were combined with the concept of the ITU (here referred to as an inter-disciplinary unit or IDU) to produce a unit culminating in a very active "Egyptian Day."

Jane J. White and Sari J. Bennett, "Frankincense and Myrrh: Solving a Mystery with Historical Geography," *Social Education* 52, no. 7 (November-December 1988): 520–26.

While this article does not technically describe an interdisciplinary unit, it provides an excellent model for developing a unit around an academic problem to be solved. The authors thoroughly describe the planning process for this type of unit.

Antoinette Worsham, "The Natural for Interdisciplinary Instruction," *Middle School Journal* 17, no. 3 (May 1986): 3, 26–27.

Thinking skills rather than content, or even themes, have provided a successful format for integrating the curriculum.

Chapter 6

TRAPS TO AVOID

In the preceding five chapters we have provided a definition of team organization, a research-based rationale for the practice, and numerous suggestions for making the most of the opportunities that teaming offers. In concluding our discussion of teaming we would like to share some insights that the authors, along with their mentor Paul George, have gained from over fifty years of combined experience with teams: teaching on them, studying them, interviewing those who work on them, conducting staff development for those beginning or extending team practice, and training preservice teachers to work on teams. We have identified eleven traps that have made team organization difficult, if not impossible, for those educators who inadvertently fell into them. Anticipating and avoiding these problems can lead to a much more satisfying experience with teaming.

1. *Failing to recognize that team organization is fundamentally different from traditional departmentalized or self-contained arrangements.*

Teaming is a "liberating" organizational structure for students, teachers, and alert administrators. It breaks down the isolation of teachers that is endemic to departmentalization and self-contained arrangements. Teaming is a structure that will allow more frequent and more profound communication to occur in school settings. As a result, educators can expect collegial decision making to become a reality in their buildings. Teachers will be able to move toward freely adapting instructional time, space, and curriculum to the needs of their students. They will also expect to have a greater say in the making of buildingwide decisions that affect their work. Teaming is much more than an alternative scheduling format. It will lead to new, more professional relationships among teachers and between teachers and administrators.

2. *Attempting to team without adequate staff development in such aspects as team skills (communications, group decision mak-*

116

ing, and organization of effective meetings) and team practices (goal setting, record keeping, evaluation).

It is sometimes falsely assumed that because teachers talk a great deal as part of their work, they don't need any assistance with communications skills when they are thrust together on teams. We must remember, though, that teachers in departmentalized or self-contained settings are seldom ever asked to work together in carrying out their daily responsibilities. If a staff development program is to prepare teachers completely for successful teaming, it must not only include an explanation of what teaming is and what it can do for teachers but also provide for hand-on teaming experiences during which teams develop common rules, orientation plans, discipline plans, and so forth. It must also anticipate that teachers will need assistance in understanding and using the skills associated with successful small groups.

3. Failing to place team organization at the top of the scheduling priority list so that all else revolves around it—and not the other way around.

If you have become convinced that team organization is an arrangement that can improve schooling for teachers and students, you must be willing to build your school master schedule around the teaming concept. You must be aware of powerful constituencies that can skew the design of the school schedule. Be alert to avoid the tracking or the stacking of teams that might create "gifted" teams, "Chapter 1" teams, or "band" teams. These situations will invariably have a negative impact on school climate. Also be alert to the potential effects of pull-out programs, which can play havoc with teacher autonomy regarding the scheduling of students within the block schedule. By all means group and re-group students *within* teams whenever it is appropriate to meet their instructional needs. However, do whatever you can to reduce or eliminate constraints on the team teachers' use of team instructional time. In summary, provide a block schedule populated with a heterogeneous group of students, and let the teachers on the team schedule students into learning experiences within the block.

4. Failing to understand that new teams will need time and practice in order to develop into fully functioning teams.

Teams are very sophisticated organizational structures. It takes several years for them to pass through the various stages of

117

teaming. This is true if teams consist of the same personnel from year to year. It is even more true if teams acquire new members along the way. Team members must get to know each other professionally and acquaint themselves with the other subjects being taught on the team before they can be expected to work closely together to coordinate the curriculum. In addition, teams will probably not spend a lot of time on student concerns until the members have developed norms and procedures to govern how they will conduct their meetings and how they will make decisions. Administrators can help teachers by showing them how to draft a time line for a reasonable growth plan. One should not expect teachers to engage in complicated interdisciplinary units during the first year of teaming. Though such practices are legitimate reasons for going to team organization, other things must happen first before teams can successfully conduct such units. Expecting the most advanced team practices too soon will primarily frustrate teachers new to teaming.

5. Failing to consider personalities and interpersonal variables when staffing teaching teams and planning for staff development.
Of all the possible education innovations that could be tried, teaming is perhaps the one most dependent on interpersonal interaction for its success. Mandating that teaming will occur simply will not suffice. It is crucial that some type of personality, leadership style, or teaching style measure be used to help with the staffing decisions and, more importantly, with the orientation of team members to one another. Devote some staff development time to affective skills as well as to the cognitive aspects of teaming. Whenever possible, keep teams together from year to year. Move personnel among teams only for specific reasons, not just to "shake things up" or "make things interesting." When moving personnel from one team to another, be sure you are doing it for the good of both teams involved in the transaction.

6. Attempting to team without choosing somebody to be responsible for the ongoing monitoring and support of teaming, which must include regular communication between teamed teachers and administrators.
It is important to establish a team leader/administrator steering committee for school decision making. The administrator who co-

ordinates the teams and convenes the team leader meetings can be the principal, the assistant principal, or a teacher who is released from the classroom part time to serve as team coordinator. The bottom line is that someone must unquestionably be in charge of coordinating the teams. In the absence of such a person, accountability is unclear, and the commitment to teaming will soon begin to slip. Develop some system of team evaluation with both internal and external aspects. Internally the teachers can monitor their own progress. Externally the administration can document the function of teaming in the school setting.

Communication with teachers not assigned to teams is critical. When parent conferences are scheduled, teams should have a system for including those staff who teach the involved student(s) and yet cannot be present at the preconference team meeting or the conference itself. Likewise, when special activities or field trips are planned, teams should keep all staff informed. The existence of a team leader steering committee is very important for ensuring that cross-team communication is ongoing.

7. *Failing to organize teams so that they are comprised of teachers with a common planning period who teach different core subjects to a common group of students in some common area of the building.*

Often the conditions for teaming are not perfect. Knowing what can be compromised and what must be held sacred is an important part of keeping the integrity of teaming intact. Common planning time cannot be violated. Sometimes the existence of odd numbers of students or the desire to staff a special class on one team will cause administrators to schedule teachers to teach students on two different teams. When this happens, that teacher almost always meets with only one of those teams during planning time. Such a teacher cannot function very well on the team that he or she does not meet with. Some schools that share faculty with another school in the district have even been known to schedule those faculty members into the second building at the same time when their team planning time has been scheduled in the first building. This practice does not work. If there is an odd number of students, it is better to create an odd-sized team of, for example, two teachers and fifty students than it is to use cross-teaming or to create a large team in which the teachers do not share all the students. The

119

requirements of common planning time and shared students can seldom be violated with impunity.

On the other hand, the block schedule can be manipulated without cutting so profoundly into the operation of the team. While the ideal situation is for a group of teachers to have an instructional block equal in length to the number of subjects taught on the team (e.g., four periods for four subjects taught), it is possible to break this full block into a couple of smaller ones without doing mortal damage to teaming. However, you do not have the luxury of going to the other extreme and asking teamed teachers to function in a traditional departmentalized schedule. There must be some time during the day when *all* the students assigned to a team are with their teamed teachers. It is even important to provide at least two back-to-back periods to facilitate instructional decision making.

Even the concept of team space can be violated to some extent for good cause without terminally damaging teaming. For example, when a school turns to team organization, it almost always does so from some other organizational pattern, such as departmentalization. Often the faculty must deal with the fact that all the science rooms for the whole school are adjacent to one another. Therefore, it is not possible to group the science teachers with the language arts, mathematics, and social studies teachers to form a contiguous team area. Even the sovereign territory of the United States is broken up because Alaska and Hawaii are not connected to the "lower forty-eight." Likewise, a team area can be "sovereign" even if it is not all contiguous.

8. Failing to understand the significance of team identity and the power of symbols, ritual, and ceremony in the life of the team.
Successful teams consciously develop identities. They create names, logos, mascots, team histories, colors, and ceremonies. Assuming that it is either unnecessary or just silly to focus on team identity will diminish the effectiveness of the team. Since these elements are highly personal and unique to individual teams, there is much variation in how specific teams go about creating team identity. Certainly, the maturity of students on the team would govern to a large extent the nature of the identity-creating process. However, successful teams create newsletters for parents, hold awards ceremonies for students, and plan special events for every-

one, all the while displaying on letterhead and in their team space some graphic symbols of their identity.

9. *Failing to integrate team organization with the rest of the school program.*

Teaming will not be very effective if it is conceived of as something tacked onto an already complicated school organization. However, when team organization is seen as the central organizing feature of a school, it can be synergetically related to other parts of the school organization. Teaming can be interwoven into the guidance program to make it easier for counselors to communicate with teachers and to better identify students who need their specialized counseling skills. Teaming can improve the decision-making procedures within the faculty. Teaming can strengthen the relationship between the regular education teachers and the special education faculty. Someone must consciously look for ways to integrate the teams into these other facets of the school program.

10. *Failing to nurture faculty esprit de corps, and failing to nurture academic departments, which retain some important functions.*

As wonderful as team organization is most of the time for its practitioners, it can lead to a different type of isolation for teachers. Instead of single teachers feeling cut off from each other, a group of four or five teachers might come to feel separated from the rest of the faculty. Consequently, faculty social functions remain very important, as do such things as schoolwide task forces and committees that meet to deal with matters of mutual concern. Chief among these areas of concern is feeling cut off from other teachers of one's own subject. Efforts must be made to periodically bring together teachers of the same subjects so that curriculum can be coordinated across grade levels and among different teachers at the same grade level.

11. *Failing to set goals for the growth and development of teams.*

Many schools begin their teaming efforts without sufficient team planning and with exceedingly ambitious expectations for first-year teams. Similarly, other schools with daily team planning begin with casually articulated goals. Two important points should be recognized: (1) teams should set goals and expectations for growth and development, and (2) these goals and expectations for team-work should be commensurate with the amount of planning time available. Reasonable first-year goals might include attention to the issues of organization, identity, and management. Later, greater attention can be devoted to instruction and evaluation. The key here is that teaming flourishes with direction and guidance.

The eleven traps addressed in this chapter have all caused grief for some unsuspecting faculties that attempted to make teaming work, only to be disappointed with the results. If you are aware of these traps and plan to avoid them, your chances of having an experience with teaming that meets your expectations will be greatly increased.

BIBLIOGRAPHY

1. Ambrose, Anthony; Blair, Mary; Brodeur, Gerri; Gerard, Carol; and Vemmer, Keith. "How We Survived the First Year of Teaming." *KAMLE Karavan: Journal of the Kansas Association for Middle Level Education* 1, no. 1 (1986–87): 16–17.

2. Arhar, Joanne M.; Johnston, J. Howard; and Markle, Glenn C. "The Effects of Teaming and Other Collaborative Arrangements." *Middle School Journal* 19, no. 4 (July 1988): 22–25.

3. _____. "The Effects of Teaming on Students." *Middle School Journal* 20, no. 3 (January 1989): 24–27.

4. Ashton, Patricia T., and Webb, Rodman B. *Making a Difference: Teachers' Sense of Efficacy and Student Achievement.* New York: Longman, 1986.

5. Barth, Roland S. "Outside Looking In—Inside Looking In." *Phi Delta Kappan* 66, no. 5 (January 1985): 356–58.

6. Beane, James A.; Toepfer, Conrad F., Jr.; and Alessi, Samuel J., Jr. "An Illustrative Interdisciplinary Resource Unit: Living in the Future." In *Curriculum Planning and Development.* Boston: Allyn and Bacon, 1986.

7. Bell, Louise C. "Learning Centers in the Classroom." *Middle School Journal* 14, no. 2 (February 1983): 17–19.

8. Blake, Robert, and Mouton, J. S. *The Managerial Grid.* Houston: Gulf Publishing, 1964.

9. Blanchard, France. "Outdoor Education As a Team Experience." *KAMLE Karavan: Journal of the Kansas Association for Middle Level Education* 1, no. 1 (1986–87): 9–12.

10. Boyer, Ernest L. *High School: A Report on Secondary Education in America.* New York: Harper & Row, 1983.

11. Brandt, Ron. "On Changing Secondary Schools: A Conversation with Ted Sizer." *Educational Leadership* 45, no. 5 (February 1988): 30–36.

12. Brodsky, Melvyn A. "The Roaring Twenties: An Interdisciplinary Unit—Or How To Make Use of That Old Raccoon Coat in the Attic." *Middle School Journal* 18, no. 4 (August 1987): 7–9.

13. Buckingham, Francine; Jordan, Lucille; and Scholl, Shirley S. "There Is No Finish Line: The Story of a Successful Interdisciplinary Unit Carried Out by 'Amateurs.'" *Middle School Journal* 18, no. 2 (February 1987): 18–19.

123

14. Clark, Sally N. "Changing the Arizona Constitution: Middle-Level Students Become Involved." *TEAM: The Early Adolescence Magazine* 3, no. 3. (January-February 1989): 14-17.

15. Daniels, Timothy; O'Brien, Joseph; and Pittman, Robert. "Interdisciplinary Units—Keystones of Learning." *Middle School Journal* 13, no. 3 (May 1982): 14-16.

16. Descamps, Jorge, and Lindahl, Ronald A. "A Classroom Management Program for the Middle School." *Middle School Journal* 20, no. 2 (November 1988): 8-9.

17. Doda, Nancy. *Teacher to Teacher.* Columbus, Ohio: National Middle School Association, 1981.

18. _____. "School Effectiveness and the Middle School: The Missing Links." Paper presented at the annual meeting of the National Middle School Association, Chicago, November 1983.

19. _____. "Teacher Perspectives and Practices in Two Organizationally Different Middle Schools." Ph. D. diss., University of Florida, Gainesville, 1984.

20. Dodd, Anne Wescott. "Try a Total School Effort To Improve Student Writing." *Middle School Journal* 16, no. 3 (May 1985): 8-10.

21. Dumpert, Bonnie S.; Sturis, Susan M.; Winfrey, Della S.; and Ennis, Scott. "Comments from an Experienced Team." *KAMLE Karavan: Journal of the Kansas Association for Middle Level Education* 1, no. 1 (1986-87): 17-18.

22. Dunning, Ernest A. "Harmony vs. Discord." *The NELMS Journal* 1, no. 2 (September 1988): 23-26.

23. Erb, Thomas O. "Structure for Openness: An Eighth Grade Unit on Exploration." *Opening Education for Children and Youth* 6, no. 2 (Winter 1979): 24-27.

24. _____. "What Team Organization Can Do for Teachers." *Middle School Journal* 18, no. 4 (August 1987): 3-6.

25. _____. "Focusing Back on the Child by Liberating the Teacher." *TEAM: The Early Adolescence Magazine* 2, no. 3 (January 1988): 10-18.

26. _____. "Planning for Successful Teaming: Common Meeting Time Is Not Enough." *Transcent Trails: Journal of the Colorado Association of Middle Level Education* 2, no. 1 (1988): 1-3.

27. Fox, Robert; Schmuck, Richard; Van Egmond, Elmer; Ritvo, Miriam; and Jung, Charles. *Diagnosing Professional Climates of Schools.* Fairfax, Va.: NTL Learning Resources Corp., 1973.

28. Garvin, James P. "A Positive Approach to Interdisciplinary Team

Organization." Paper presented at the annual meeting of the National Middle School Association, St. Louis, November 1987.

29. George, Paul S. "Interdisciplinary Team Organization: Four Operational Phases." *Middle School Journal* 13, no. 3 (May 1982): 10–13.

30. _____. "Research on Effective Teams." Paper presented at the annual meeting of the National Middle School Association, Denver, November 1988.

31. George, Paul, and Lawrence, Gordon. *Handbook for Middle School Teaching.* Glenview, Ill.: Scott, Foresman, 1982.

32. George, Paul S., and Oldaker, Lynn L. *Evidence for the Middle School.* Columbus, Ohio: National Middle School Association, 1985.

33. Glasser, William. *Schools Without Failure.* New York: Harper & Row, 1969.

34. Goodlad, John I. *A Place Called School: Prospects for the Future.* New York: McGraw-Hill, 1984.

35. Gregorc, Anthony F. *Gregorc Style Delineator.* Maynard, Mass.: Gabrial Systems, 1978.

36. _____. *An Adult's Guide to Style.* Maynard, Mass.: Gabrial Systems, 1982.

37. Guild, Pat Burke, and Garger, Stephan. *Marching to Different Drummers.* Alexandria, Va.: Association for Supervision and Curriculum Development, 1985.

38. Hall, Gene E.; Loucks, Susan F.; Rutherford, William L.; and Newlove, Beulah N. "Levels of the Use of the Innovation: A Framework for Analyzing Innovation Adoption." *Journal of Teacher Education* 24, no. 1 (1975): 52–56.

39. Hall, Gene E., and Rutherford, William L. "Concerns of Teachers About Implementing Team Teaching." *Educational Leadership* 34, no. 3 (1976): 227–33.

40. Hass, Mary E. "Learning from an Old Mail-Order Catalogue: A Resource Unit on Change in America." *Middle School Journal* 19, no. 2 (February 1988): 22–24.

41. Hord, Shirley M.; Rutherford, William L.; Huling-Austin, Leslie; and Hall, Gene E. *Taking Charge of Change.* Alexandria, Va.: Association for Supervision and Curriculum Development, 1987.

42. Humphreys, Alan H.; Post, Thomas R.; and Ellis, Arthur K. *Interdisciplinary Methods: A Thematic Approach.* Santa Monica, Calif.: Goodyear Publishing Co., 1981.

43. James, Michael. *Adviser-Advisee Programs: Why, What, and How.* Columbus, Ohio: National Middle School Association, 1986.

44. Johnson, David W.; Johnson, Roger T.; Holubec, Edythe J.; and Roy, Patricia. *Circles of Learning: Cooperation in the Classroom.* Alexandria, Va.: Association for Supervision and Curriculum Development, 1984.

45. Johnston, J. Howard; Markle, Glenn C.; and Arhar, Joanne M. "Cooperation, Collaboration, and the Professional Development of Teachers." *Middle School Journal* 19, no. 3 (July 1988): 28–32.

46. Johnston, J. Howard, and Ramos de Perez, Maria. "Four Climates of Effective Middle Level Schools." In *Schools in the Middle: A Report of Trends and Practices.* Reston, Va.: National Association of Secondary School Principals, 1985.

47. Jung, Carl G. *Psychological Types.* 1921. Reprint. Princeton, N.J.: Princeton University Press, 1971.

48. Keirsey, David, and Bates, Marilyn. *Please Understand Me: Character and Temperament Types.* Del Mar, Calif.: Prometheus Nemesis Book Co., 1984.

49. Kerble, Marc. "Incorporating Special Education Teachers into Teams: Why and How?" *Middle School Journal* 19, no. 4 (July 1988): 18–19.

50. Kerekes, Joanne. "The Interdisciplinary Unit...It's Here To Stay." *Middle School Journal* 18, no. 4 (August 1987): 12–14.

51. Kierstead, Janet. "Direct Instruction and Experiential Approaches: Are They Really Mutually Exclusive?" *Educational Leadership* 42, no. 8 (May 1985): 25–30.

52. _____. "How Teachers Manage Individual and Small-Group Work in Active Classrooms." *Educational Leadership* 44, no. 2 (October 1986): 22–25.

53. Kolb, David. *Learning Style Inventory.* Boston: McBer and Co., 1976.

54. Kolb, David; Rubin, Irwin M.; and McIntyre, James M. *Organizational Psychology: An Experiential Approach.* 3d ed. Englewood Cliffs, N.J.: Prentice-Hall, 1979.

55. Lawrence, Gordon. *People Types and Tiger Stripes: A Practical Guide to Learning Styles.* Gainesville, Fla.: Center for Applications of Psychological Type, 1981.

56. Levy, Phyllis S. "Webbing: A Format for Planning Integrated Curricula." *Middle School Journal* 11, no. 3 (August 1980): 26–27.

57. Lipsitz, Joan. *Successful Schools for Young Adolescents.* New Brunswick, N.J.: Transaction Books, 1984.

58. Little, Judith Warren. "Norms of Collegiality and Experimentation:

Workplace Conditions of School Success." *American Educational Research Journal* 19, no. 3 (Fall 1982): 325–40.

59. Merenbloom, Elliot Y. *The Team Process in the Middle School: A Handbook for Teachers.* 2d ed. Columbus, Ohio: National Middle School Association, 1986.

60. Myers, Isabel Briggs. *Introduction to Type.* Palo Alto, Calif.: Consulting Psychologists Press, 1962.

61. _____. *Gifts Differing.* Palo Alto, Calif.: Consulting Psychologists Press, 1980.

62. Myers, Isabel Briggs, and Briggs, Katherine C. *Myers-Briggs Type Indicator.* 1943. Reprint. Palo Alto, Calif.: Consulting Psychologists Press, 1976.

63. Pickler, Gene. "The Evolutionary Development of Interdisciplinary Teams." *Middle School Journal* 18, no. 2 (February 1987): 6–7.

64. Pinot, Rene, and Emory, Ruth. *Preparing Education Training Consultants.* Portland, Oreg.: Northwest Regional Education Laboratory, 1975.

65. Purkey, William. *Self-Concept and School Achievement.* Englewood Cliffs, N.J.: Prentice-Hall, 1970.

66. Rosenholtz, Susan J. "Political Myths About Educational Reform: Lessons from Research on Teaching." *Phi Delta Kappan* 66, no. 5 (1985): 349–55.

67. Sharan, Shlomo. "Cooperative Learning in Small Groups: Recent Methods and Effects on Achievement, Attitudes, and Ethnic Relations." *Review of Educational Research* 50, no. 2 (Summer 1980): 241–71.

68. Sizer, Theodore. *Horace's Compromise: The Dilemma of the American High School.* Boston: Houghton Mifflin, 1984.

69. Slavin, Robert E. *Cooperative Learning: Student Teams.* Washington, D.C.: National Education Association, 1982.

70. _____. *Using Student Team Learning.* 3d ed. Baltimore: Team Learning Project, The Johns Hopkins University, 1986.

71. _____. "Ability Grouping and Student Achievement in Elementary Schools: A Best-Evidence Synthesis." *Review of Educational Research* 57, no. 3 (Fall 1987): 293–336.

72. Soar, Robert, and Soar, Ruth. "An Attempt To Identify Measures of Teacher Effectiveness from Four Studies." *Journal of Teacher Education* 27, no. 3 (Fall 1976): 261–67.

73. Streit, M. Jill, and Schnurstein, Carol D. "The Journal of the Team-

ship Holmes: Survival in an Interdisciplinary Habitat." *Middle School Journal* 15, no. 2 (February 1984): 18–21.

74. Stromberg, Robert B., and Smith, Joan M. "The Simulation Technique—Applied in an Ancient Egypt I.D.U." *Middle School Journal* 18, no. 4 (August 1987): 9–11.

75. Tye, Kenneth A., and Tye, Barbara B. "Teacher Isolation and School Reform." *Phi Delta Kappan* 65, no. 10 (1984): 319–22.

76. Vars, Gordon F. *Interdisciplinary Teaching in the Middle Grades.* Columbus, Ohio: National Middle School Association, 1987.

77. _____. "Maintaining Order in the Classroom: The Use of a Discipline Ladder and Asking Yourself Four Key Questions May Help." *Middle School Journal* 20, no. 2 (November 1988): 4–6.

78. White, Jane J., and Bennett, Sari J. "Frankincense and Myrrh: Solving a Mystery with Historical Geography." *Social Education* 52, no. 7 (November-December 1988): 520–26.

79. Whitehead, Alfred N. *The Aims of Education.* New York: Mentor Books, 1963.

80. Williams, E. Craig. "Now You're Talking, It's Team Time." *KAMLE Karavan: Journal of the Kansas Association for Middle Level Education* 2, no. 1 (1987–88): 11–12.

81. Worsham, Antoinette. "The Natural for Interdisciplinary Instruction." *Middle School Journal* 17, no. 3 (May 1986): 3, 26–27.